„Wenn dein Schiff brennt, gehst du nicht ins Bett!“

Hapag-Lloyd
Kapitäne
im Porträt

“When your ship is on fire, you can’t just go to bed!”

Profiles of
Hapag-Lloyd
Captains

Text / Texts:
Ulrike Fischer

Fotos / Photography:
Axel Martens

Inhalt
Contents

Liebe Leserinnen und Leser,

der weltweite Handel ist ohne die Schifffahrt nicht denkbar. Rund 90 Prozent aller Handelsgüter werden auf dem Seeweg transportiert. Containerreedereien wie Hapag-Lloyd sind existenziell für den globalen Handel – und ebenso existenziell für den sicheren und reibungslosen Transport von Gütern sind unsere Seeleute.

Ob Wiper oder Ingenieur:in, Auszubildende oder Chief Mate, Wachoffizier:in oder Köchin/Koch – und natürlich unsere Kapitäninnen und Kapitäne – sie alle sorgen dafür, dass unsere Container wohlbehalten und pünktlich an ihrem Bestimmungsort ankommen. Zwar haben moderene Technologien die Seewege sicherer gemacht, aber die Naturgewalten der Ozeane stellen selbst erfahrene Seeleute regelmäßig vor große Herausforderungen.

Wer sind die Menschen, die sich mit so viel Leidenschaft ihrem Beruf

Dear readers,

Global trade is unimaginable without shipping, as roughly 90 per cent of all goods traded worldwide are transported by sea. Container shipping companies like Hapag-Lloyd are crucial to global trade – and our seafarers are just as crucial to the safe and smooth transport of goods.

Whether wiper or engineer, apprentice or chief mate, officer of the watch or cook – and, of course, our captains – they all ensure that our containers arrive at their destination safely and on time. Although modern technologies have made sea routes safer, the natural forces of the oceans regularly pose major challenges even to experienced seafarers.

Who are these people who are so passionately devoted to their profession? What drives them to sail for months on end far from friends and family? In this book, 15 Hapag-Lloyd captains – including one female captain – share their stories.

hingeben? Was treibt sie an, monatelang unterwegs zu sein, weit weg von Familien und Freunden? In diesem Buch kommen 14 Kapitäne und eine Kapitänin von Hapag-Lloyd zu Wort. Sie berichten von beschwerlichen und unbeschwerten Reisen, von Glücksgefühlen auf hoher See und unvergessenen Begegnungen irgendwo auf der Welt. Sie nehmen uns mit durch den Suezkanal oder auf die Werften in China, und gewähren dabei sehr persönliche Einblicke in ihr Leben an Bord, ihre Erfahrungen und Werte. Es sind ganz unterschiedliche Charaktere, die aber eines verbindet: ihre allumfassende Liebe zur Seefahrt.

Mein herzlicher Dank gilt allen hier Porträtierten für die Bereitschaft, ihre Erfahrungen auf See mit Ihnen, liebe Leserinnen und Leser, zu teilen. Aber er gilt auch allen anderen unseren Seeleuten, die Tag für Tag, Nacht für Nacht, dafür sorgen, dass unsere Schiffe sicher die Ozeane durchqueren und wohlbehalten die Häfen der Welt anlaufen können. Ihnen allen gilt mein und unser aller Respekt und unsere Hochachtung.

Ich wünsche Ihnen eine unterhaltsame Lektüre.

Rolf Habben Jansen
Vorstandsvorsitzender Hapag-Lloyd AG

They tell of voyages both arduous and carefree, of feelings of contentment on the high seas, and of unforgettable encounters at various places across the world. They take us along through the Suez Canal or to the shipyards in China, providing very personal insights into their life on board, their experiences and their values. Despite their very different personalities, they all share one thing in common: a profound love of seafaring.

My heartfelt thanks go out to all the captains profiled here for their willingness to share their experiences at sea with you, the readers. But I must also express my thanks to all our other seafarers, who ensure – day after day, night after night – that our ships cross the oceans safely and can call at ports around the world in sound condition. Each of them deserves the respect and high regard of both myself and all of us.

I hope you enjoy reading these profiles!

Rolf Habben Jansen
CEO Hapag-Lloyd AG

Endlich Kapitän!

Jonathan Pompe

Finally a captain!

Im Juni 2020 wurde Jonathan Pompe zum Kapitän befördert – hier erzählt er, wie man vom Segelboot aufs Containerschiff kommt, was er auf seiner ersten Fahrt als Kapitän erlebte und warum er mit seiner Familie nach Malaysia zieht.

Jonathan Pompe was promoted to captain in June 2020. Here, he shares how he transitioned from sailboats to container ships, how his first voyage as a captain went, and why he and his family are moving to Malaysia.

Angekommen: Die Seefahrt habe ihn selbstbewusster gemacht, erzählt Jonathan Pompe beim Treffen am Container Terminal Altenwerder

Arrived: Seafaring has made him more self-confident, Pompe says during our meeting at Hamburg's Container Terminal Altenwerder

<<

Kaum wurde er zum Kapitän befördert, schon ging es fünf Monate am Stück auf große Fahrt: „Vancouver, Japan, Singapur, Halifax, dann wieder rüber nach Singapur und noch mal zurück nach Halifax, das war schon eine lange Zeit“, erzählt der 35-Jährige. Corona hat so manchen Fahrplan beeinflusst – Jonathan Pompe nimmt's gelassen. „Ich hatte hinterher genauso lange frei“, erzählt er an Bord der „Kyoto Express“ am Hamburger Container Terminal Altenwerder. „Außerdem fahre ich sehr gern den Asiendienst. Ich mag die asiatische Lebensweise – und meine Frau kommt aus Singapur“, fügt er hinzu. Morgen um 5.30 Uhr geht es Richtung Indien. Diesmal für knapp drei Monate, wenn nichts dazwischenkommt.

Am Anfang war der Baggersee

Jonathan Pompe hat die Liebe zur Seefahrt auf Südsee entdeckt. Aber nicht vor Hawaii, sondern auf dem gleichnamigen

Right after being promoted to captain, he set sail on a long voyage that would last five months. "Vancouver, Japan, Singapore, Halifax, then back over to Singapore and back to Halifax – that was one long voyage," the 35-year-old says. The coronavirus was notorious for the impact it had on sailing schedules, but Jonathan Pompe is able to shrug it off. "I still had just as much time off work after I got back," he says on board the "Kyoto Express", which is berthed at the Container Terminal Altenwerder in Hamburg. "On top of that, I really enjoy sailing in the Asia service. I like the Asian way of life – and my wife is from Singapore," he adds. In any case, he and his ship will be setting sail tomorrow at 5:30 in the morning. And, this time, the voyage will be for just under three months – unless, of course, something unexpected comes up.

Baggersee in Braunschweig nahe der Autobahn. Hier lernte der damals Fünfjährige mit seinem Zwillingsbruder segeln. „Wir waren so oft auf dem Wasser, wie es ging, erst mit kleinen Optimisten, später auf Jollen, Katamaranen, Lasern, auf allem, was unser Braunschweiger Segelverein so hergab. Mein Zwillingsbruder und ich haben dann als Jugendliche das Training der Jüngeren übernommen. Auf den vielen Törns auf der Ostsee habe ich auch die großen Schiffe bestaunt." Zur See fahren, das wäre doch was, dachte sich der Schüler damals. Eine Besichtigung der alten „Hamburg Express" im Hamburger Hafen gab den letzten Kick. „Ich bewarb mich dann nach der Schule direkt für die Ausbildung zum Schiffsmechaniker." Seinem Vater habe er das erst nach der Zusage von Hapag-Lloyd gebeichtet: „Er hätte mich gern als Optiker in einem seiner beiden Läden gesehen. Aber ich wollte raus und auf eigenen Beinen stehen – heute ist er stolz auf mich", freut sich Kapitän Pompe. In Leer studierte er nach seiner gut zweieinhalbjährigen Ausbildung Nautik, dann ging es schnurstracks auf See und von Rang zu Rang nach oben.

Taifun vor Hongkong

Seinen ersten richtigen Sturm erlebte Jonathan Pompe als junger Wachoffizier vor Hongkong. „Das war mit Kapitän Van der Hoff, der damals seine erste Reise auf der ‚Stuttgart Express' absolvierte. Wir lagen an der Werft, als sich ein Taifun ankündigte, und mussten auf Anweisung der Behörden sofort raus aus dem Hafen, die Angst vor Beschädigung durch losgerissene Schiffe ist dort sehr groß. Regen, Sturm und hohe Wellen empfingen uns auf dem offenen Meer, es wurde eine lange Nacht für alle. Wir hatten keine Ladung an Bord und das Schiff reagierte sehr instabil. Wir versuchten zu ankern,

Beginnings on an artificial lake

Pompe didn't discover his love for seafaring in some romantic spot, such as on the North Sea or off Hawaii. Instead, he found it on Südsee, a man-made lake near an autobahn in the central German city of Brunswick. Here, he learned how to sail with his twin brother when they were 5 years old. "We were on the water as often as we could, first with small Optimists, later on Jollyboats, catamarans and Lasers – in other words, on everything that our local sailing club had to offer. Then, once we were teenagers, my twin brother and I took over the training of the younger sailors. And, of course, I also watched the big ships during my many sailing trips on the Baltic Sea."

I wanted to get out and stand on my own two feet

Though still in high school at the time, the young man thought that seafaring might be a career worth pursuing. But what pushed him over the edge was a tour he took of the old "Hamburg Express" in the Port of Hamburg. "Right after graduating from high school, I applied for an apprenticeship to qualify as a ship mechanic," he says, adding that he only shared this with his father once his application at Hapag-Lloyd had been accepted. "He would have liked me to be an optician in one of his two stores. But I wanted to get out and stand on my own two feet – and today he is proud of me," Captain Pompe says with a smile. After a two-and-half-year apprenticeship, he studied Nautical Sciences at the University of Applied Sciences Emden/Leer in north-western Germany. And then he went straight to sea, where he climbed the ranks.

Typhoon off Hong Kong

Pompe encountered his first real storm as a young officer of the watch off Hong

aber aufgrund des schlechten Wetters hielt der Anker zunächst nicht, das klappte erst nach mehreren Versuchen. Am nächsten Morgen hatte sich die See beruhigt. Wir zogen den Anker wieder hoch, und mit ihm unzählige Fischernetze und Drähte, die sich in der Kette verfangen hatten. Es dauerte eine Weile, um alles zu beseitigen."

Ich wollte raus und auf eigenen Beinen stehen

Eine ungewöhnliche erste Abfahrt als Kapitän

Und wie war es, in Vancouver das erste Mal als Kapitän abzulegen? „Ich war ein bisschen angespannt, aber auch superkonzentriert. Leider hatte sich die Hafenreihenfolge durch Corona so verändert, dass ich nur eine kurze Übergabe im Hafen von Vancouver bekam. Aber die ‚Kyoto Express' kenne ich noch aus meiner Ausbildungszeit und war auch schon als Schiffsmechaniker hier tätig – jetzt das Sagen zu haben, das ist schon ein großartiges Gefühl. Ein paar Tage später erkrankte der Chief Engineer plötzlich. Ich dachte erst, er hätte eine Blutvergiftung. Später stellte sich heraus, dass er sich im Flieger eine Thrombose zugezogen hatte. Also drehten wir wieder um – so habe ich in meiner ersten Woche als Kapitän auch gleich medizinische Erstversorgung gemacht und mein erstes Ankermanöver vor Vancouver ausgeführt." Da kein Ersatz für den erkrankten Seemann verfügbar war, übernahm der Zweite Ingenieur. „Aber gut fünf Wochen später kam unser Chief Engineer in Kuala Lumpur wieder an Bord. Wir haben uns sehr gefreut, dass es ihm wieder gut ging und wir wieder vollständig waren."

Jonathan Pompe muss auf seiner ersten Kapitänsfahrt einiges richtig

Kong. "That was with Captain Van der Hoff, who was on his first voyage on the 'Stuttgart Express' at the time. We were moored at the quay when a typhoon started approaching. The authorities instructed us to leave the port immediately, as there is a lot of fear there about damage caused from ships breaking loose. Once out on the open sea, we were greeted by rain, storms and high waves – and it ended up being a very long night for everyone. We didn't have any cargo on board, and the ship reacted very unstably. We tried to anchor ourselves. But due to the bad weather, the anchor didn't take hold at first, and we were only firmly anchored after several attempts. By the next morning, the sea had calmed down. So we pulled up the anchor – along with the countless fishing nets and wires that had got caught in our anchor chain. It took us a while to untangle everything."

An unusual first departure as captain

When asked about his first time casting off as a captain, Pompe says: "I was a bit tense, but also super-focused. The coronavirus had unfortunately changed our port rotation, so I only received a very brief handover in the Port of Vancouver. But I am familiar with the 'Kyoto Express' from my days as an apprentice, and I also worked on it as a ship mechanic. So it's a great feeling to be in charge of it now. In any case, a few days after casting off, the chief engineer suddenly fell ill. At first, I thought he had blood poisoning. But we later learned that he had actually developed a thrombosis on the plane. So we had to turn back. This means that in my first week as captain, I also performed medical first aid and did my first anchor manoeuvre off Vancouver." As no

Schon als Azubi fuhr er auf der „Kyoto Express", jetzt als Kapitän. „Fühlt sich an wie nach Hause kommen", sagt Jonathan Pompe

He has sailed on the "Kyoto Express" – as an apprentice and now as a captain. "It feels like coming home," Pompe says

>>

Die Zukunft? Liegt in Malaysia. Im Juli 2021 zog Familie Pompe nach Johor Bahru nördlich von Singapur

Where does his future lie? In Malaysia! In July 2021, the Pompe family moved to Johor Bahru, north of Singapore

gemacht haben, denn für die zweite Fahrt haben bereits einige Besatzungsmitglieder wieder angeheuert. „Ich mag es familiär, unterhalte mich gern mit den Leuten, meine Tür stand auch als Chief Mate immer offen", erklärt er seinen Führungsstil. Klar müsse man kontrollieren, ob jeder seinen Job auch gut erledigt. „Aber ich mache das mehr so nebenbei, komme mal auf einen Schnack zu den Leuten. Niemand soll das Gefühl haben, dass ich ihm auf die Finger schaue." Sein Selbstbewusstsein und seine Offenheit hätten sich aber erst mit der Zeit entwickelt. „Früher war

replacement was available for the seafarer who had fallen ill, the second engineer took charge. "But our chief engineer came back on board a bit over five weeks later in Kuala Lumpur. We were thrilled that he was well again and that we were whole again as a crew."

Pompe must have done something right on his first voyage as a captain, as some crew members from it have already signed on to join his second voyage. "I like to keep things family-like and to talk with people. Even when I was chief mate, I always kept my door open," he says in

ich eher schüchtern und zurückhaltend, aber die Seefahrt verändert dich. Wenn man viel rumkommt, lernt man auch viel kennen. Heute liebe ich den Small Talk, freu mich, wenn Kundinnen und Kunden an Bord kommen und ich mit ihnen eine Führung machen kann. Und ich glaube, es liegt auch an meiner Frau. Ich bin internationaler geworden durch sie."

______ Asien – die große Liebe

Kennengelernt hat er seine Frau Sheue Wei als junger Schiffsmechaniker in Singapur. „Ich fuhr für eine Reederei, die auf Schwergut spezialisiert war. Drei Wochen lagen wir dort vor Anker. Eines Abends besuchte ich dann beim Landgang die legendäre „Raffles Bar" auf einen Drink, da sind wir uns zum ersten Mal begegnet. Als der Kapitän mitbekam, dass ich jemanden kennengelernt hatte, gab er mir auch mal tagsüber frei. So konnten Sheue Wei und ich mehr Zeit miteinander verbringen – und verliebten uns." Das ist zehn Jahre her und Innenarchitektin Sheue Wei zog nach zwei Jahren Fernbeziehung für ihre große Liebe nach Braunschweig. Die Kinder Karolina und Konstantin sind sechs und fast ein Jahr alt, und nach anfänglichem Fremdeln mit den Schwiegereltern versteht sich Sheue Wei mit ihnen so gut, dass sie sogar bei der Innengestaltung des Optikerladens geholfen hat. Längst spricht sie fließend Deutsch. Ihre Urlaube verbrachte die junge Familie meist in Südostasien. Nicht nur um Verwandte zu besuchen, sondern auch um Land und Leute zu erkunden. „Wir reisen wahnsinnig gern, Backpacking mit Kindern ist großartig! Außerdem mag ich die asiatische Mentalität, die Offenheit, mit der die Menschen einander begegnen. Da muss man sich nicht zum Kaffee verabreden, man kommt einfach vorbei."

Und das könnte in Zukunft öfter passieren, denn die Pompes ziehen mit

describing his leadership style. Of course, he adds, you have to check to make sure that everyone is doing their job well. "But I do that more in passing by dropping by for a brief chat with people. No one should have the feeling that I'm watching them like a hawk." Nevertheless, it takes time for this kind of self-confidence and openness to develop. "I used to be rather shy and reserved, but seafaring changes you. When you get around a lot, you also get to know a lot. These days, I love small talk, and I'm happy when customers come on board and I can give them a tour. Plus, I think I owe that a bit to my wife. She has made me more cosmopolitan."

______ Asia – his great love

Pompe met his future wife, Sheue Wei K., in Singapore when he was a young ship mechanic. "I was working for a shipping company that specialised in heavy lift cargo. We were lying at anchor there for three weeks. Then, while on shore leave one evening, I stopped by the legendary Long Bar in the Raffles Hotel for a drink. And that's the first time we encountered each other. When the captain found out that I had met someone there, he gave me some time off during the day. That made it possible for Sheue Wei and me to spend more time together – and to fall in love."

That was a decade ago. But after two years of a long-distance relationship, Sheue Wei – an interior designer – moved to Brunswick for the love of her life. They now have two children: Karolina, who is six, and Konstantin, who is almost a year old. After some mutual shyness at first, Sheue Wei now gets on so well with her in-laws that she even helped her father-in-law to redesign the interiors of his stores. For some time now, she has spoken fluent German. The young family has usually spent its holidays in South-East Asia – not only to visit relatives, but also to explore

Vom Kapitän zum Kunden – für den Umzug nutzen auch die Pompes die Containerschifffahrt

From captain to customer – the Pompes are also using container shipping for the move

Kind und Kegel nach Malaysia. „Mein Schwiegervater braucht mehr Hilfe und wir haben beschlossen, auch mal in der Heimat meiner Frau zu leben. Wir ziehen nach Johor Bahru gleich oberhalb von Singapur, da ist das Leben entspannt und günstiger. Karolina freut sich auch schon auf unseren neuen Lebensabschnitt, sie spricht dank meiner Frau auch Mandarin." Jonathan Pompe wird die Containerschifffahrt jetzt erstmals als Kunde kennenlernen, denn Möbel, Haushaltsgeräte und Spielzeug werden im Sommer in einem Container die Reise antreten. Hapag-Lloyd will er in jedem Fall treu bleiben, kann sich auch vorstellen, mal als Joker einzuspringen, wenn in Singapur kurzfristig ein Kapitän gebraucht wird. Auf seinen Arbeitgeber lässt der gut gelaunte Mann ohnehin nichts kommen: „Hapag-Lloyd ist eine der besten deutschen Reedereien. Von der Verpflegung und dem Leben an Bord, über die 1:1-Regelung beim Fahren bis hin zu einer einzigartigen und harmonischen Zusammenarbeit zwischen Schiff und Land. Das gibt es so bei keiner anderen Reederei!"

the countries and cultures. "We are crazy about travelling, and backpacking with a child is simply fantastic! What's more, I like the Asian mindset, the openness with which people interact with each other. There, you don't make a date to have coffee with people – you just drop by."

And this could be happening more often starting in July, as that's when the entire Pompe family will be pulling up stakes and moving to Malaysia. "My father-in-law needs a bit more help and we decided to live in my wife's home country for a change," Captain Pompe says. "We are moving to Johor Bahru, just across from Singapore, where life is more relaxed and less expensive. Karolina is also looking forward to this new phase of our life, and she also speaks Mandarin thanks to my wife."

Pompe will now learn about container shipping from a customer's perspective, as all of the family's furniture, household appliances and toys will be starting their voyage to Malaysia this summer in a container. In any case, he plans to stay true to Hapag-Lloyd, and he can also imagine being able to step in as a substitute if a captain is needed at short notice in Singapore.

Regarding his employer, the good-natured man only has positive things to say: "Hapag-Lloyd is one of the best German shipping companies. This includes the provisions and life on board, the 1:1 time-on/time-off rule for sailing, and the unique and well-harmonised collaboration between its employees on land and at sea. You won't find that with any other shipping company!"

Was macht Jonathan Pompe heute?

Die vergangene Fahrt war recht anstrengend, schreibt Jonathan Pompe per E-Mail: „Wir retteten erst eine Segelyacht im Indischen Ozean, dann ein Flüchtlingsboot im Mittelmeer. Alles ist gut gegangen." In Malaysia hat sich seine Familie bestens eingelebt. „Karolina geht in die zweite Klasse und ist super glücklich. Sie lernt Deutsch, Englisch, Mandarin und Spanisch. Wahnsinn, wie schnell Kinder Sprachen lernen! Konstantin geht in den Kindergarten, meine Frau meistert so viel in der Zeit, in der ich auf See bin. Danke, Sheue Wei!"

What's Jonathan Pompe doing today?

The past voyage was quite exhausting, Pompe writes via email: "We first rescued a sailing yacht in the Indian Ocean, then a refugee boat in the Mediterranean. Everything turned out fine." In Malaysia, his family has settled in perfectly. "Karolina is in second grade and is super happy. She is learning German, English, Mandarin and Spanish. It's amazing how quickly children learn languages! Konstantin is attending kindergarten, and my wife handles so much while I'm at sea. Thank you, Sheue Wei!"

CONTAIN

Von Flucht, Courage und Piraten

Gebhard Knull

Of escape, courage and pirates

41 Jahre fuhr Gebhard Knull zur See, machte noch die „Ochsentour" vom Schiffsjungen bis zum Matrosen, wie er seine Lehrzeit in den 1950ern bezeichnet. Als Offizier und Kapitän fuhr er für Hapag-Lloyd große und kleine Schiffe rund um die Welt. Von der Liebe zur Seefahrt seit Kindertagen, Zoff mit Vorgesetzten, Piraterie im Chinesischen Meer und wie er zu seinem Spitznamen „K-Zero" kam, erzählt er im „Internationalen Maritimen Museum Hamburg".

Retired Captain Gebhard Knull spent 41 years at sea as a cabin boy, officer and master. At the International Maritime Museum Hamburg he speaks about quarrels with superiors, the love of seafaring, piracy in the China Sea, and how he came to be nicknamed "K-Zero".

Gebhard Knull liebt die Seestücke des Künstlers Johannes Holst. Hier mit einer Vergrößerung von „Anatomie einer Welle" im Internationalen Maritimen Museum

Knull loves the seascape paintings by the artist Johannes Holst. Here he is with an enlargement of "Anatomy of a Wave" in Hamburg's International Maritime Museum

<<

Schon auf meiner ersten Fahrt habe ich fast alles erlebt, was die Seefahrt so spannend macht", erzählt Gebhard Knull und berichtet von der Flucht über die Ostsee auf einem kleinen Küstenmotorschiff (Kümo) im Januar 1945. „Mein Vater hatte in Königsberg – heute Kaliningrad – den Auftrag, Flüchtlinge mit Schiffen zu evakuieren. Er schickte auch meine Mutter und uns vier Brüder mit einem Kümo Richtung Westen. In der ersten Nacht stand ich mit meinem Bruder auf der Back, das ist der Aufbau auf dem Vorschiff. Als der Ausgucker rief ‚Fahrzeug vier Strich backbord', sahen wir schemenhaft ein Schiff direkt auf uns zukommen und verließen die Back. Aber das Deck war so vereist, dass wir ausrutschten und genau dahin schlitterten, wo uns das Schiff dann rammte. Wir konnten den Bug himmelhoch über uns sehen!", erinnert sich der 88-Jährige.

Beeindruckt hat den jungen Gebhard Knull damals vor allem der

Starting with my first voyage, I experienced nearly everything that makes seafaring so exciting," says Gebhard Knull, recounting his escape across the Baltic Sea on a small coaster in January 1945. "My father had the job in Königsberg, today's Kaliningrad, of evacuating refugees on ships. He also sent my mother and us four brothers on a coaster. That first night, I stood on the foredeck with my brother. When the lookout shouted, 'Vessel four points on the port side,' we saw a shadowy ship coming straight at us and ran from the foredeck. But the deck was so icy that we slipped and slid right to the place where the ship rammed us. We were lying on deck and could see the bow towering right over us!" the 88-year-old remembers.

Young Knull was most impressed by the captain at the time. "He reassured

Kapitän. „Er beruhigte uns, es sei nichts Schlimmes passiert, wir könnten alle unter Deck gehen. In Pillau (Baltijsk) wurde das Schiff repariert, in Gotenhafen (Gdynia) sollte unsere Mutter dann mit uns vier Söhnen auf die ‚Wilhelm Gustloff' umsteigen. Aber sie weigerte sich und wir blieben an Bord des Kümos – so hat sie uns höchstwahrscheinlich das Leben gerettet." Die „Wilhelm Gustloff" sank nach dem Beschuss durch ein sowjetisches U-Boot am 30. Januar 1945. An Bord über 10.000 Menschen, von denen nur 1.239 überlebten. Mutter Knull und ihre vier Söhne erreichten nach vierwöchiger Überfahrt auf dem Kümo Sassnitz. Alle vier Brüder fuhren später zur See.

Die Tipps des Vaters verschafften Respekt

Die ersten Berufstipps bekam Gebhard Knull von seinem Vater: „Erstens: Als Schiffsjunge musst du kochen und die Kombüse putzen! Merke dir: Wenn die Ecken und Winkel eines Raumes sauber sind, ist der ganze Raum sauber. Zweitens: Ein Wenn und Aber gibt es nicht an Bord. Drittens: ‚Geht nicht' gibt's auch nicht, man findet immer einen Weg. Zuletzt: Halt deinen Namen im Gespräch!" Besonders der letzte Rat habe sich bewährt, resümiert Gebhard Knull. Gibt's ein Beispiel? Kapitän Knull lacht und erzählt: „Das war später beim Norddeutschen Lloyd. Ich war Zweiter Offizier auf der ‚Birkenstein' und für die Ladung zuständig. In Hamburg luden wir Bierfässer, in Antwerpen kamen 30 Kartons mit gepressten Schwämmen dazu. Als wir in New York die Ladung löschen wollten, quollen uns diese zu Tausenden entgegen. Die Fässer hatten sich gelöst und die Kartons beschädigt. Die Schwämme haben wir mit einem riesigen Tuch rausgehievt und schnell in den Schuppen gebracht. Nachmittags zitierte mich der Kapitän an Deck und

us all that nothing bad had happened, and that we could all go below deck. The ship was repaired in the Russian seaport town of Baltiysk, and our mother was supposed to transfer to the 'Wilhelm Gustloff' with her four sons in Gotenhafen [Gdynia]. But she refused, so we stayed on board the coaster – and she most likely saved our lives." In fact, the "Wilhelm Gustloff" sank after being fired on by a Russian submarine on 30 January 1945. Only 1,239 of the more than 10,000 people on board survived. Mother Knull and her four sons arrived at Sassnitz after a four-week crossing on the coaster. All four brothers later went to sea.

If we hadn't acted with such discipline and calm, people could have been killed!

Tips from his father help him to earn respect

Knull got his first professional tips from his father: "First of all, as a cabin boy, you have to cook and clean the galley! Remember: if the nooks and crannies of a room are clean, the whole room is clean. Second: there are no 'ifs and buts' on board. Third: there's no such thing as 'can't' – you can always find a way. And finally: keep your name in the conversation!" Knull sums up that this last piece of advice has proved particularly valuable. When asked for an example, Knull laughs and says: "It happened later, at North German Lloyd. I was a second officer on the 'Birkenstein' and responsible for the cargo. In Hamburg, we loaded beer barrels; in Antwerp, we added 30 cartons of pressed sponges. When we went to unload the cargo in New York, thousands of sponges swelled out at us. The barrels had come loose and damaged

machte mich zur Schnecke, weil er fünf Schwämme in der Luke entdeckt hatte. Als er drohte, dass er mir das ins Zeugnis schreiben würde, platzte mir der Kragen, und ich wurde genauso laut wie er: ‚Wenn im Zeugnis irgendetwas Ehrenrühriges steht, sehen wir uns vor Gericht!' Wir führten ein lebhaftes Wortgefecht, bis er sich plötzlich zum Ersten Offizier umdrehte und sagte: ‚So was möchte ich einmal von Ihnen erleben! Guten Tag, meine Herren' – und verschwand. Ab da hatte ich ein ausgezeichnetes Verhältnis zum Kapitän. Die Geschichte sprach sich bis zur Reederei herum, ich hatte mir Respekt verschafft."

Wenn wir nicht so diszipliniert und ruhig gehandelt hätten – es hätte Tote geben können!

Piratenangriff!

1958 erlebte Gebhard Knull als Steuermann seinen ersten Piratenangriff. „Wir lagen mit der ‚Buchenstein' vor Buenaventura in Kolumbien vor Anker. Der Mond schien, von Land wehte die Musik vom Vergnügungsviertel herüber und wir ärgerten uns, dass wir Wache schieben mussten. Der Kapitän hatte mir eingeschärft, den gegenüberliegenden Mangrovenwald im Blick zu behalten. Wenig später kam aus dem Wäldchen tatsächlich ein Einbaum mit acht Männern gefahren und nahm Kurs auf uns. Ich schickte den Wachmann auf die Back mit dem Befehl, den Ankerklüsendeckel fallen zu lassen, sobald der erste Pirat raufklettern wollte. Kurze Zeit später hörte ich ein dumpfes Plopp und wie der Kerl ins Wasser stürzte. Die Piraten kehrten um. Ich schoss zur Abschreckung noch mit der Signalpistole hinterher."

the cartons. We heaved the sponges out with a huge cloth and quickly brought them to the shed. In the afternoon, the master summoned me on deck and bawled me out because he'd found five sponges in the bay. When he threatened to write me up for what happened, I blew my top and fired back: 'If you report anything defamatory about me, we'll see each other in court!' We had a lively exchange of words until he suddenly turned to the chief officer and said: 'I'd like to see you do something like this! Good day, gentlemen.' And then he disappeared. From then on, I enjoyed an excellent relationship with the master. The story spread all the way to the shipping company. I was respected now."

Pirate attack!

In 1958, Knull experienced his first pirate attack as a helmsman. "We were anchored with the 'Buchenstein' off Buenaventura in Colombia. The moon shone brightly, music wafted across from the entertainment district, and we were irritated that we had to keep watch. The master had told me to keep an eye on the mangrove forest opposite. A little later, a dugout canoe with eight men came out of the forest and headed straight for us. I sent the watchman to the foredeck with the order to drop the anchor hawse flap as soon as the first pirate tried to climb up. A short time later, I heard a dull plop as the guy fell into the water. The pirates turned around. I took a farewell potshot at them with the signal pistol as a deterrent."

After the 1970 merger of HAPAG with North German Lloyd, which created Hapag-Lloyd AG, Knull sailed as a chief officer until he received his appointment as captain in 1973. "I was lucky enough to sail my first voyage on the

Geschichtenerzähler: In der Piratenecke des Internationalen Maritimen Museums Hamburg kennt sich der Kapitän bestens aus

Storyteller: The captain knows his way around the section of the International Maritime Museum Hamburg dedicated to piracy

>>

Gebhard Knull mit einem der berühmten „Knochenschiffe" aus der Ära der Napoleonischen Kriege. Französische Gefangene fertigten die kunstvollen Modelle aus Tierknochen

Knull with one of the famous "bone ships" from the era of the Napoleonic Wars. French prisoners used animal bones to make these intricate models

^

Nach der Fusion des Norddeutschen Lloyds mit der HAPAG zur Hapag-Lloyd AG 1970 fuhr Gebhard Knull als Erster Offizier, bis er 1973 seine Ernennung zum Kapitän erhielt. „Ich hatte das Glück, meine erste Reise auf der ‚Birkenstein' zu fahren, ein Frachter, den ich wirklich in- und auswendig kannte."

Kapitänszeit, wie sie im Buche steht

1975 wurde Kapitän Knull Nautischer Inspektor, vier Jahre später Vice President Operations bei der Agentur U.S. Naviga, (später Hapag-Lloyd America) in New

'Birkenstein', a cargo ship I really knew inside out," he says.

A textbook career

In 1975, Captain Knull became a nautical inspector, and four years later he was Vice President Operations at the U.S. Naviga agency (later Hapag-Lloyd America) in New York. Only then did he switch back to seafaring. At 1.90 metres tall, he sailed for five years on what was then the smallest container ship, which Hapag-Lloyd had chartered out to a Japanese shipping company. "That was the 'Windward', with 970

York. Erst dann wechselte der 1,90-Meter-Mann wieder zur Seefahrt und fuhr fünf Jahre auf dem damals kleinsten Containerschiff, das Hapag-Lloyd an eine japanische Reederei verchartert hatte. „Das war die ‚Windward' mit 970 TEU. Es ging von Japan über Hongkong bis zur Westküste Australiens, nach Freemantle, und wieder zurück. Diese Route hat mir auch deshalb so gut gefallen, weil ich in jeder Hinsicht eigenständig handeln konnte. Eine Kapitänszeit wie sie im Buche steht!", erzählt Gebhard Knull. Dass er in dieser Zeit Windanfälligkeit und Treibstoffverbräuche der „Windward" mit diversen Tests dokumentierte, bescherte ihm einen Schiffswechsel: Er übergab seine „Forschungsergebnisse" in der Vorstandsetage. Wenig später erhielt er das Kommando über die noch in Shanghai im Bau befindliche „Berlin Express".

_____"Five minutes! Money – or I kill you!"
Und auf eben dieser erlebte Kapitän Knull mit seiner Mannschaft im August 1991 einen Piratenangriff, der sogar Schlagzeilen in der Tagespresse schrieb. „Es war nachts um eins. Wir fuhren bei gutem Wetter durch die Straße von Malakka Richtung Singapur. Der Lotse hatte einige Stunden Verspätung, also reduzierten wir die Geschwindigkeit. Es war viel Verkehr, der Wachoffizier und ich hatten auf der Brücke zu tun. Gegen 1.15 Uhr sollte der Wachwechsel stattfinden, der Ablöser reagierte aber nicht auf den Telefonanruf. Wir schickten den Ausguck zur Kontrolle nach unten. Er entdeckte, dass meine Kabine aufgebrochen war und meldete es. Als wir dann gemeinsam runtergingen, trafen wir im Gang auf zwei mit Macheten und Pistolen bewaffnete Piraten. ‚You, Captain! Five minutes! Money or I kill you!', riefen sie. Drei weitere kamen dazu, den Schiffbetriebsoffizier als Geisel vor sich herschiebend. Ich dachte in diesem

TEU. It went from Japan via Hong Kong to Freemantle, on the west coast of Australia, and back again. I really enjoyed this route because I could be independent in every respect and was my own master. A textbook master's experience!" Knull says. During this time, he documented the wind susceptibility and fuel consumption of the "Windward" by means of various tests. This earned him a change of ship when he handed over his "research results" in the boardroom. A short time later, he was given command of the "Berlin Express", which was still under construction in Shanghai.

_____"Five minutes! Money – or I kill you!"
On the "Berlin Express", Captain Knull and his crew experienced a pirate attack in August 1991 that even made headlines. "It was one o'clock in the morning, and we were sailing in good weather through the Strait of Malacca towards Singapore," he recounts. "The pilot was a few hours late, so we reduced speed. There was a lot of traffic on the move, and the watch officer and I were busy on the bridge. At about 1:15 a.m., the change of watch was supposed to take place, but the shift relief didn't respond to our phone call. We sent the lookout below to check. He discovered that my cabin had been broken into and reported it. When we went down together, we were confronted in the corridor by two pirates armed with machetes and pistols. 'You, captain! Five minutes! Money – or I kill you!' they shouted. Three more joined them, pushing the ship's operations officer in front of them as a hostage. All I could think of in that moment was: 'Keep calm.' Together, we went to my cabin. But there were only 325 marks and the on-board handcuffs in my safe. The pirates took my watch, officer's knife and pen, and handcuffed me. The situation was tense; they wanted more. Since they

Moment nur: ‚Ruhe bewahren'. Gemeinsam gingen wir zu meiner Kabine. Aber in meinem Safe befanden sich nur 325 Mark und die bordeigenen Handschellen. Die Piraten nahmen mir Uhr, Offiziersmesser und Kugelschreiber ab und legten mir die Handschellen an. Die Lage war angespannt, sie wollten mehr. Da sie außer ihrer Sprüche kein Englisch konnten, war es schwierig, ihnen klarzumachen, dass das meiste Geld im Safe des Schiffsbüros lag. Irgendwie schaffte ich es und lotste sie dorthin. Den Safe räumten sie dann komplett leer und erbeuteten um die 10.000 Mark. Außerdem nahmen sie alles mit, was von Wert war. Schließlich scheuchten sie uns aufs Heck, fesselten uns aneinander und verschwanden an Seilen über die Reling in das zehn Meter tiefer liegende Boot. Der Piratenboss verschwand als Letzter mit einem lachenden ‚No problem, Captain' – der Spuk war vorbei!" Kapitän Knull ist sicher: „Wenn wir alle nicht so diszipliniert und ruhig gehandelt hätten – es hätte Tote geben können!"

K-Zero

Und wie kam er nun zu seinem Spitznamen K-Zero? „Das war damals in New York", erzählt Gebhard Knull und lächelt: „Als ich mich einem amerikanischen Kollegen vorstellte, fragte er mich, was mein Name auf Englisch bedeute. Ich sagte nur: ‚K is K and null means zero' – da hatte ich meinen Spitznamen weg."

didn't know any English apart from their commands, it was hard to make them understand that most of the money was in the ship's office safe. Somehow I managed to guide them there. They emptied the safe completely and got away with about 10,000 marks. They also took everything of value. Finally, they shoved us along and onto the stern, tied us together and disappeared on ropes over the railing into a boat waiting 10 metres below. The pirate boss was the last to disappear, laughing, 'No problem, Captain,' and the nightmare was over!" Knull ends the story saying with certainty in his voice, "If we hadn't all acted with such discipline and calm, people could have been killed!"

K-Zero

So how did he get his nickname "K-Zero"? "It was back in New York," Knull recounts with a smile. "When I introduced myself to an American colleague, he asked me what my name meant in English. I just said, 'K is K, and null means zero.' And that's how I got my nickname."

Was macht Gebhard Knull heute?

Mit seinen 88 Jahren erfreut sich Gebhard Knull bester Gesundheit und gibt gern noch ein paar Tipps für zukünftige Kapitäninnen und Kapitäne: „Unabhängig vom seemännischen Können sollte ein Kapitän vor allen Dingen ein gutes Selbstbewusstsein besitzen, sei es vor Reedereimitarbeitern, Abladern, Agenten, Stauern oder sonstigen Leuten, die mit dem Schiff zu tun haben. Ferner muss er entscheidungsfreudig und bereit sein, kalkulierbare Risiken einzugehen. Der Besatzung gegenüber sollte er fair und gerecht sein, kritische Entscheidungen treffen können, auch wenn diese manchmal unbequem sein mögen." Aye, aye, Käpten!

What's Gebhard Knull doing today?

At the age of 88, Knull is in good health and still likes to give a few tips to aspiring captains: "Apart from seafaring skills, a captain should most importantly have good self-confidence, be it in front of shipping company employees, shippers, agents, clearance officers, stevedores and other people who have something to do with the ship. On top of that, they must also be decisive and willing to take calculable risks. They should be fair and just to the crew and be able to make tough decisions, even if they may be uncomfortable at times." Aye, aye, captain!

200

HHLA
CTA
CAPTAIN

Durch die Ankerklüse an die Spitze

Andrew Longnecker

Through the anchor hawse to the top

Als junger Mann angelte Andrew Longnecker vor Alaska Lachs und Kabeljau mit seinem eigenen Schiff. Auf einem Containerriesen umzusteigen, sah er als große Chance, mehr aus seinem Leben zu machen. Heute ist er sehr stolz darauf.

As a young man, Andrew Longnecker fished for salmon and cod off Alaska on his own boat. He saw switching to a giant container ship as a great opportunity to make more of his life. Today, he is very proud of it.

„Welcome aboard!" Andrew Longnecker auf der „Philadelphia Express" im Container Terminal Altenwerder in Hamburg

"Welcome aboard!" Andrew Longnecker on the "Philadelphia Express" in Hamburg's Container Terminal Altenwerder

<<

Keine Frage, die „Philadelphia Express" sah schon bessere Tage. Das 3237-TEU-Containerschiff hat 18 Jahre auf dem Buckel, hier und da erzählt ein bisschen Rost davon und ja, auch der Schriftzug könnte mal erneuert werden. Aktuell ist der Aufzug defekt, was nicht weiter schlimm ist, denn die Crew ist jung und fit und flitzt gern die Treppen rauf und runter. Andrew Longnecker lässt nichts auf sein Schiff kommen. „Ich kenne die ‚Philadelphia Express' in- und auswendig, jede Ecke, jede Reparatur – es ist einfach ein großartiges Gefühl, alles über ein Schiff zu wissen", erzählt der 53-jährige Amerikaner. Seine Route geht von Hamburg über London, Charleston, Port Everglades nach Houston und dann zurück über Savannah, Norfolk, Antwerpen wieder nach Hamburg. „Der Atlantische Ozean hat auf dieser Strecke einiges an Stürmen zu bieten", berichtet der Kapitän. Zehn, zwölf Meter hohe Wellen seien nichts Außergewöhnliches. „Bei

Without a doubt, the "Philadelphia Express" has seen better days. The 3,237 TEU container ship has 18 years under its belt. It's a bit rusty in places and, yes, the lettering could also use a bit of touching up. The lift isn't working right now. But that isn't such a big deal, as the crew is young and fit, and they like to race up and down the stairs. Plus, Andrew Longnecker won't stand any criticism of his ship. "I know the 'Philadelphia Express' inside out – every corner, every repair. It's just a great feeling to know everything about a ship," says the 53-year-old American.

The route will meander from Hamburg to London, Charleston, Port Everglades and Houston, and then back to Hamburg via Savannah, Norfolk and Antwerp. "The Atlantic Ocean has a lot of storms to offer on this stretch," the

mitlaufender See ist das halb so wild, aber wenn du den Sturm und 4000 Seemeilen vor dir hast, brauchst du viel Erfahrung. Auch die Hurrikan-Saison vor der Ostküste im Spätsommer ist nicht ohne. Gerade letztes Jahr kamen wir vor Charleston einem Hurrikan sehr nahe, ein zweiter kam dazu. Aber dann verzog sich der eine nach Norden, der andere Richtung Süden – wir hatten Glück!"

______ Aufwachsen an der Ostküste, Angeln vor Alaska

„Mein Vater fuhr zur See, meine zwei Schwestern und ich sind quasi an Bord vor der Ostküste aufgewachsen", erzählt Andrew Longnecker. „Nach der Highschool bin ich dann nach Alaska gezogen, um in der Hochseefischerei zu arbeiten. Ich landete bei einer norwegischen Fischerfamilie. Deren Longliner waren aus Holz, wurden von Generation zu Generation vererbt. Wenn du damit in schwere Wetter kommst, biegen sich buchstäblich die Planken, du wirst nass bis auf die Knochen, kriegst kaum Schlaf. Das Fischen mit Langleinen ist schwere körperliche Arbeit – aber als junger Mann habe ich es geliebt!", erzählt der Kapitän. Mit 26 kaufte er sich sein eigenes Schiff: „Die ‚Virginia Creeper', ein gut 22-Meter-Longliner. Großaugen Thunfisch, der bis zu zweieinhalb Meter groß wird, Kabeljau, Schwertfisch – bis zu 15 verschiedene Arten haben wir bei Wind und Wetter aus dem Meer geholt", erzählt Andrew Longnecker mit leuchtenden Augen. Damals lebte er auf Hawaii, wo er auch seine spätere Frau kennenlernte. Und wie kommt man von der Fischerei auf ein Containerschiff? „Einige meiner Freunde hatten schon die Seiten gewechselt, ihre Lizenz gemacht und fuhren als Dritte Offiziere auf Frachtern. So sehr ich die Fischerei mochte, mir wurde durch unsere Gespräche klar, dass die Containerschifffahrt

captain notes, adding that waves up to 10 or 12 metres high are nothing out of the ordinary. "It isn't so bad when you're sailing with the current, but when you have the storm and 4,000 nautical miles ahead of you, you need a lot of experience. And the hurricane season off the East Coast in late summer isn't without its challenges, either. Just last year, we came very close to a hurricane off Charleston, and a second one came in after that. But then one headed north and the other south. We just got lucky!"

______ Growing up on the East Coast, fishing off Alaska

"My father was a seafarer, and my two sisters and I more or less grew up on board off the East Coast," he recounts. "Then, after high school, I moved to Alaska to work in deep-sea fishing. I ended up with a Norwegian fishing family. Their wooden longliners were passed down from generation to generation. When you run into rough weather on one of these boats, the planks literally bend, you get soaked to your bones, and you hardly get a wink of sleep. Longline finishing is tough, physical work – but as a young man, I loved it," the captain says.

At 26, he bought his own boat. "The 'Virginia Creeper', a good 22-metre longliner. Bigeye tuna, which grow to up to two-and-a-half metres, cod, swordfish – we brought up to 15 different species out of the water in all weathers," Longnecker fondly recalls.

At the time, he was living in Hawaii, where he also met his future wife. When asked how he went from fishing to container shipping, he says: "Some of my

Showing the guys how the job works is very fullfilling

mehr Zukunft hat, besonders, wenn du eine Familie gründen willst."

Verwechslung ausgeschlossen: Auch die Sicherheitshelme verraten den Dienstgrad

Mix-ups are impossible: Safety helmets also indicate rank

^
^

Rang für Rang an die Spitze, und dann dem Nachwuchs zeigen, wie es geht

„Ich habe mich vom einfachen Seemann bis zum Kapitän hochgearbeitet. Wir Amerikaner nennen das Hawsepiper", erklärt der Kapitän. Das sei einer, der an der Ankerkette durch die Klüse aufs Schiff klettert. 2009 startete er als Dritter Offizier erst auf der „St. Louis Express", dann der „Washington Express", bis er auf der „Philadelphia Express" landete. Hier wurde er Chief Mate und erhielt 2017 sein Kapitänspatent. Die ganze Familie sei unglaublich stolz auf seine Beförderung gewesen, so Longnecker. „Besonders mein Vater. Ich nahm ihn mal ein Stück bis nach Norfolk mit, weil er noch nie auf einem so großen Schiff gefahren ist. Da sagt er zu mir: ‚Du hast meine Leidenschaft geerbt und sie in deine Karriere verwandelt'."

So sehr Kapitän Longnecker das Abenteuer liebt, heute gilt seine Leidenschaft der Ausbildung junger Leute. „Den Jungen zu zeigen, wie der Job funktioniert, sie zu begleiten und zu beobachten, wie sie an ihren Aufgaben wachsen, das ist sehr erfüllend", findet der hochgewachsene Mann: „Ich habe hier einen Kollegen an Bord, den kenne ich noch aus der Zeit, als ich selbst Chief Mate war. 18 Monate hatte er in Afghanistan gedient, bevor er hier als Kadett anfing, mittlerweile ist er Zweiter Offizier. Ich bin stolz, ihn auf seinem Weg begleiten zu können!"

Aber mal ehrlich: Ist es nicht auch ein bisschen langweilig, immer auf

friends had already switched over, gotten their licence and sailed as third officers on cargo ships. As much as I liked fishing, I realised through our conversations that container shipping offered more of a future, especially if you want to start a family."

Climbing to the top, and then showing young people how it's done

"I worked my way up from ordinary seaman to captain. We Americans call it being a hawsepiper," the captain says, explaining that it refers to someone who climbs onto the ship through the hawse of the anchor chain – or, less figuratively, someone who did not attend a traditional maritime college or academy to earn an officer's licence, but did so by accumulating enough sea time and taking the necessary training courses and exams.

Longnecker got his start in 2009 as a third officer, sailing on the "St. Louis Express" and the "Washington Express" until he ended up on the "Philadelphia Express". He became a chief mate on this ship and then earned his master's license in 2017. His entire family was incredibly proud of his promotion, Longnecker says, adding: "Especially my dad. I once took him along for a bit up to Norfolk because he'd never been on a ship that big before. That's when he said to me, 'You inherited my passion and turned it into your career.'"

As much as Captain Longnecker loves adventure, he is passionate these days about training the younger generation. "Showing the guys how the job works, monitoring their progress and watching them grow in their roles is very fulfilling," the tall captain says. "I have a colleague here on board whom I've known ever since I was a chief mate myself. He had served 18 months in Afghanistan before he started here as a cadet, and now he's

Goodbye, America! Mittlerweile fährt die „Philadelphia Express" als „Spartel Trader" unter liberischer Flagge

Goodbye, America! The "Philadelphia Express" now sails under the Liberian flag as the "Spartel Trader"

>>

CLU 01842
561

demselben Schiff zu fahren? „Überhaupt nicht!", protestiert Andrew Longnecker. „Es ist toll, eine Route häufig zu fahren. Denn einerseits hast du eine gewisse Kontinuität, andererseits immer wieder neue Leute an Bord. Jede Fahrt ist anders." Die Stürme seien das eine, und die „Philadelphia Express" sei auch schon mal in angedocktem Zustand gerammt worden, was ihr ein paar Werfttage einbrachte. „Aber es passieren eben auch Dinge wie vor ein paar Jahren, als wir im Golf von Mexiko ein Rettungsboot mit kubanischen Geflüchteten entdeckten. Vier Männer und eine hochschwangere Frau in einem winzigen Boot. Wir haben sie sicher bis zur nächsten Küstenwache gelotst."

Den Jungen zu zeigen, wie der Job funktioniert, ist sehr erfüllend

______ Vielfalt in Bremerhaven, Zeit für Familie in Charleston

Die Crew der „Philadelphia Express" kommt aus der ganzen Welt. „Honduras, Türkei, Indonesien, Ghana, um nur einige Länder zu nennen. Und jede:r hier an Bord hat seine eigene Geschichte. Gerade heute morgen unterhielt ich mich mit einem indonesischen Offiziersanwärter. Er lebt in Wisconsin, erzählte mir aber sehnsüchtig von seiner Heimat Bali und der wunderbaren Natur. Bei der Seefahrt lernst du eben nicht nur andere Häfen und Länder kennen, auch an Bord ist das manchmal wie eine Weltreise!"

Kapitän Longnecker kann allen Häfen etwas abgewinnen, sogar Bremerhaven, den die „Philadelphia Express" bis vor zwei Jahren anlief. „Auch wenn mancher das belächeln mag – ich finde es schön, wenn man das Gefühl hat, nach Hause zu kommen. Wir kennen die Stadt, wissen, wo man gut essen und einkaufen

a second officer. I'm proud to be able to accompany him on his journey!"

But let's be honest: Doesn't it also get a bit boring to always sail on the same ship? "Absolutely not!" Longnecker responds defensively. "It's great to frequently sail a single route. On the one hand, you have a certain continuity; on the other, you always have new people on board. Every voyage is different."

And then you also have storms, he explains, and the "Philadelphia Express" has also been rammed while berthed, which forced it to spend a few days in dry dock. "But then you have things like what happened a few years ago, when we encountered a lifeboat full of Cuban refugees in the Gulf of Mexico," he recounts. "Four men and a very pregnant woman in a tiny boat. We safely escorted them to the nearest coastguard station."

______ Diversity in Bremerhaven, family time in Charleston

The crew of the "Philadelphia Express" comes from all over the world. "Honduras, Turkey, Indonesia and Ghana, to name just a few of the countries," Longnecker says. "And everyone here on board has their own story. Just this morning, I was talking with one of our Indonesian officer cadets. He lives in Wisconsin, but he was telling me how much he misses his homeland, Bali, and the wonderful nature there. When you sail, you don't just get to know other ports and countries; sometimes just being on board is also like a trip around the world!"

Captain Longnecker has something positive to say about all ports, even Bremerhaven, which the "Philadelphia Express" called at until two years ago. "Even if some people might poke fun at it, it's nice to feel like you're coming home. We know the city well, and we know where the good places to eat and shop are. I even

kann. Ich besitze sogar einen Bierkrug mit dem Schriftzug von Bremerhaven.“ Charleston, wo er mittlerweile mit seiner Frau Marta und den beiden Söhnen Nicolas und Jacob lebt, sei natürlich etwas hübscher, räumt der Familienmensch Longnecker ein: „Wir haben wunderbare Strände und die Stadt atmet ganz viel Geschichte. Wenn ich zu Hause bin, machen wir oft Ausflüge, gehen zum Beispiel wandern in die Berge. Oder ich bastle mit den Jungs etwas in meiner Werkstatt. Zuletzt haben wir eine Hantelbank gebaut – das hat Riesenspaß gemacht.“

Wenn ihn die Sehnsucht nach dem Ozean packt, schaut Kapitän Longnecker sich gern den einen oder anderen der vielen Hapag-Lloyd-Filme auf YouTube an: „Da leistet die Marketingabteilung ganze Arbeit. Jedes Mal, wenn ich diese Filme anschaue, bin ich hinterher noch stolzer, hier zu arbeiten. Meine Frau lacht dann immer und fragt: ‚Na, willst du schon wieder los?‘“

have a beer mug with the emblem of Bremerhaven on it.”

But, of course, Longnecker finds there is a lot more beauty in Charleston, where he lives with his wife, Martha, and his two sons, Nicolas and Jacob. “We have wonderful beaches, and the city exudes a lot of history,” he says. “When I'm home, I take a lot of trips with my family, such as to go hiking in the mountains. Or I make something with my boys in my workshop. We recently built a weight bench, which was a whole lot of fun.”

„I love Bremerhaven“: Kapitän Longnecker besitzt sogar einen Bierkrug aus der eher unscheinbaren Stadt

“I love Bremerhaven”: Captain Longnecker even owns a beer stein from this rather unspectacular city

When he misses the ocean, Captain Longnecker likes to watch a few of the many Hapag-Lloyd films that can be found on YouTube. “The Marketing department does a great job on them. Every time I watch them, I'm even prouder to work here,” he says. “My wife always laughs and asks: ‘Well, do you already want to get going?’”

Was macht Andrew Longnecker heute? Der sympathische Kapitän meldet sich Ende September 2022 von der ehemaligen „Al Hilal“: „Wir haben sie im August 2021 zur ‚Missouri Express‘ umgeflaggt. Das Schiff ist sehr schön und leistungsstark und es passt ordentlich was drauf!“ Zwar seien während der Umflaggung fünf Besatzungsmitglieder an Corona erkrankt und mussten eine Woche in einem Hotel in Florida in Quarantäne verbringen – „aber es ist alles gut gegangen! Und im April hab ich mit meiner Familie drei Wochen Urlaub in Portugal gemacht. Wir haben Verwandte dort und verbrachten eine tolle Zeit miteinander.“

What's Andrew Longnecker doing today? The amiable captain will report to the former “Al Hilal” at the end of September 2022: “We reflagged her as the ‘Missouri Express’ in August 2021. The ship is very beautiful and powerful – and you can fit a lot on it!” Of course, he notes, five crew members fell ill with COVID during the reflagging and had to spend a week in quarantine in a hotel in Florida. “But it all went well!” he adds. “And in April, I spent three weeks on holiday in Portugal with my family. We have relatives there and had a great time together.”

Hapag-Lloyd
CTA
71
71

Ein Kapitän, der seine Crew durch Zuhören führt

Torben Cordes

A captain who leads his crew by listening

Torben Cordes sprüht nur so vor Begeisterung, sobald er von seinem Beruf erzählt. Und das liegt möglicherweise auch an den Kapitänen bei Hapag-Lloyd, die ihm die Seefahrt beibrachten. „Ohne diese Förderung wäre ich heute nicht da, wo ich bin", erzählt der gebürtige Brunsbütteler. Kapitän auf Probe wurde er 2020 auf der „Santos Express", danach folgte die Beförderung. Was er von seinen Vorbildern gelernt hat, wie er die Mannschaft auch in schwierigen Zeiten bei Laune hält und worauf er nicht verzichten kann, wenn er nach Hause kommt, erzählt er hier.

Torben Cordes sparkles with enthusiasm as soon as he talks about his job. And that may also be due to the captains at Hapag-Lloyd who taught him seafaring. "Without their support, I wouldn't be where I am today," says the Brunsbüttel native. He became a probationary captain on the "Santos Express" in 2020 and was later promoted. Here, he tells us what he learned from his role models, how he keeps the crew happy even in difficult times, and what he can't do without when he gets home.

Küstenkind: Torben Cordes wuchs am Nord-Ostsee-Kanal auf und lebt heute mit seiner Frau im Alten Land an der Elbe

Coastal child: Cordes grew up near the Kiel Canal and now lives with his wife in the Altes Land region on the Elbe river

<<

Kapitän Torben Cordes ist ein echtes Küstenkind: aufgewachsen in Dithmarschen am Nord-Ostsee-Kanal, der Vater ein begeisterter Segler, im Freundeskreis der Familie Lotsen, Seefahrer und Wasserschutzpolizisten. „Ich habe schon in die Freundschaftsbücher in der Grundschule als Berufswunsch Kapitän geschrieben", erzählt der 38-Jährige. Trotzdem bewarb er sich nach dem Abitur erst mal zum Polizeistudium in Kiel. „Das hatte viel mit meiner Jugendarbeit im Sportverein und beim Deutschen Roten Kreuz zu tun. Die Vorstellung, als Polizist gesellschaftlich meinen Beitrag zu leisten, das hat mich gereizt!" Ein Sportunfall kam dazwischen und so durfte er das Studium nicht antreten – im Nachhinein eine glückliche Fügung, wie er findet. „Danach fuhr ich zweigleisig: In Elsfleth schrieb ich mich als Student für Nautik ein und startete das sechsmonatige Praxissemester, in Hamburg bewarb ich mich zeitgleich bei Hapag-Lloyd für

Captain Torben Cordes is a true "coast child". He grew up in Dithmarschen on the Kiel Canal, his father an enthusiastic sailor, and the family's circle of friends included pilots, sailors and water police officers. "I already wrote 'captain' as my dream job in the friendship books in elementary school," the 38-year-old says. Nevertheless, after graduating from high school, he first applied to study in Kiel to become a police officer. "That had a lot to do with my youth work in the sports club and the German Red Cross," he explains. "The idea of making my contribution to society as a police officer appealed to me!" A sports accident intervened and prevented him from starting his studies – in retrospect a lucky coincidence, he thinks. "After that, I took a two-track approach: I enrolled as a student of Nautical Sciences in Elsfleth and started

die Ausbildung zum Schiffsmechaniker." Mitten im Praktikum – Torben Cordes fuhr für die Reederei Rörd Braren auf dem Mehrzweckfrachter „Bremer Anna" – lud ihn Hamburgs Traditionsreederei zum Bewerbungsgespräch ein. „Ich bin an der Brunsbütteler Schleuse ausgestiegen, zum Ballindamm gefahren und hinterher wieder an Bord gegangen." Die Zusage kam kurze Zeit später. „Wohl auch, weil die gleich gesehen haben, dass da jemand wirklich fahren will", so der Kapitän. Das Praxissemester auf See möchte er nicht missen. „Ich war damals der einzige Deutsche an Bord des Trampschiffs, Bordsprache war gefühlt nur Russisch und ich verstand eigentlich nur ‚Dawei, dawei', was so viel wie ‚Los, los!' heißt. Kreuz und quer ging es über die Nord- und Ostsee. Holz, Papier, Baumstämme, Paletten mussten wir selbst laschen, also Ladeluken auf und rein mit dem Zeug! Und wenn du dann vor Schweden oder Finnland mit dem Schiff einfrierst und der Eisbrecher dich freischaufeln muss – das waren schon beeindruckende Erlebnisse. Eine harte Schule insgesamt, aber für mich genau richtig!"

Begegnung mit einem Riesen, Sandsturm vor Damietta

Vom 90 Meter langen Mehrzweckfrachter ging es zur Ausbildung bei Hapag-Lloyd auf die fast viermal so große „Chicago Express". Torben Cordes: „Als ich das erste Mal im Maschinenraum stand, war ich überwältigt. Und erst recht oben auf der Brücke – ich konnte mir gar nicht vorstellen, wie man so einen Riesen steuern sollte. Aber unser Kapitän Bernd Etzien sagte nur: ‚Das schaffen wir schon' und nahm uns unter seine Fittiche. Ihm habe ich unendlich viel zu verdanken!" Die Augen des Kapitäns leuchten, als er von den ersten Landgängen mit seinem damaligen Chef in Singapur berichtet: „Er fuhr mit uns zum Fischkaufen in seinen Lieblings-

the six-month internship semester. And I applied to Hapag-Lloyd in Hamburg at the same time to train to become a ship's mechanic."

It only works together and when everyone pulls together

While Cordes was sailing for the shipping company Rörd Braren on the multipurpose freighter "Bremer Anna" during his internship, Hapag-Lloyd invited him for an interview. "I got off at Brunsbüttel lock, went to the Ballindamm and got back on board afterwards," he says. The acceptance letter came a short time later. "Probably also because they saw right away that I was someone who really wanted to sail," the captain says. Even so, he didn't want to leave before finishing his practical semester at sea. "At the time, I was the only German on board the tramp steamer, the only language spoken on board was Russian, and all I really understood was 'Davai, davai!', which means 'Come on! Come on!' We sailed across the North Sea and the Baltic Sea. We had to lash wood, paper, tree trunks and pallets ourselves, so we opened the hatches and loaded the stuff! And when your ship froze up off Sweden or Finland and the icebreaker had to dig you out, those were some impressive experiences. A tough school overall, but just right for me!"

A giant sandstorm off Damietta

From the 90-metre-long multipurpose freighter, it was off to training with Hapag-Lloyd on the "Chicago Express," which is almost four times as big. "When I stood in the engine room for the first time, I was overwhelmed," Cordes says. "And even more so up on the bridge, as I couldn't imagine how to steer such a

An der Elbe wartet das familiäre Empfangskomitee, wenn der Kapitän mit dem Schiff einläuft: Dann winken Eltern und Patenkind, Frau und Großeltern

On the Elbe, his family waits as a reception committee when the captain arrives with his ship. Everyone waves to him, including his godchild, wife, parents and grandparents

laden, wo er uns dem Besitzer vorstellte und wir erst mal einen Kaffee bekamen. Wir fühlten uns akzeptiert, auch wenn wir nur Azubis waren!"

Bernd Etzien war es auch, der ihn vor zwei Jahren ermunterte, sich um die Beförderung zu kümmern. „Er sagte nur: ‚Torben, du kannst das, und wenn du es wirklich willst, unterstütze ich dich!' Diese Mischung aus Geben und Nehmen, aus Fördern und Fordern und die Erkenntnis, dass es nur gemeinsam geht: „Das habe ich von Kapitän Etzien, aber auch von den Kapitänen Uwe Fiedler und Krzystof

giant. But our captain, Bernd Etzien, just said 'We'll manage' and took us under his wing. I owe him an immense debt of gratitude!" The captain's eyes light up as he recounts his first shore excursions with his then-boss in Singapore: "He took us fish shopping at his favourite shop, where he introduced us to the owner and we first had a coffee. We felt accepted even though we were just trainees!"

It was also Captain Etzien who encouraged him three years ago to try to become a captain himself. "He just said: 'Torben, you can do this. And if you really

Kaplon gelernt“, berichtet Torben Cordes. Kapitän Kaplon ist ihm in dieser Hinsicht in bester Erinnerung: „2018, als ich noch Chief Mate war, gerieten wir mit der „Hannover Express“ vor Damietta in einen heftigen Sandsturm. Wir konnten die Hand vor Augen kaum sehen, wurden praktisch gesandstrahlt. Sechs Schlepper versuchten uns an die Pier zu kriegen, vergeblich. Und schon beim Einlaufen musst du durch den sehr engen Kanal manövrieren“, berichtet Torben Cordes: „Plötzlich sagte Kapitän Kaplon ‚Chief Mate, ich gehe einen Moment rein, Du übernimmst.‘ – Nach kurzer Zeit war er natürlich wieder da und wir haben uns dann abgewechselt, sodass wir nicht beide draußen im Sandsturm stehen mussten und einer von der Brücke aus unterstützen konnte. Dass er mir zutraute, diese Situation, auch wenn es nur wenige Minuten waren, allein zu meistern – stark! Gemeinsam haben wir dann das Schiff sicher in den Hafen gebracht.“

______ Herausforderung angenommen! Erst Kapitän auf Probe, dann rein in den Sturm

Verantwortung zu übernehmen, das hat Torben Cordes schon immer Spaß gemacht. Ob als Klassensprecher, in der Jugendgruppe oder im Sportverein. „Ich kümmere mich gern um Leute, mag es, wenn ein gutes Gemeinschaftsgefühl entsteht – und okay, ich bin auch gern Chef“, grinst der Kapitän. Im Mai 2020 stellte er genau das auf der „Santos Express“ unter Beweis. „Wir waren auf dem Weg von Cartagena nach Caucedo, als unser Kapitän erkrankte“, erzählt Torben Cordes. „Er hatte nichts Ernsthaftes, aber zur Sicherheit musste er ins Krankenhaus. Die ganze Reise über hatten wir schon Witze gemacht, weil ich mit meiner Neugier mehr in seinem Büro als in meinem war. Kurz vor Santo Domingo saßen wir dann zusammen und er sagte: ‚Torben, wir haben

want it, I'll support you!',” Cordes says. “This mixture of give and take, of being encouraging and demanding, and the realisation that it can only be done together – I learned that from Captain Etzien, but also from Captains Uwe Fiedler and Krzystof Kaplon.”

Cordes then recounts a story involving Captain Kaplon, saying: “In 2018, when I was still chief mate, we got caught in a violent sandstorm with the ‘Hanover Express’ off Damietta. We could hardly see our hand in front of our eyes, and we were practically being sandblasted. Six tugs tried to get us to the pier, but it was all in vain. And even when you're coming in, you have to manoeuvre through the very narrow channel. Suddenly, Captain Kaplon said: ‘Chief mate, I'm going in for a moment. You take over.’ He was back after a short time, of course, and then we took turns so that we didn't both have to stand outside in the sandstorm and one of us could provide support from the bridge. The fact that he trusted me to deal with this situation by myself, even if it was only for a few minutes – that was fantastic! Together, we then brought the ship safely into port.”

______ Challenge accepted!

Cordes has always enjoyed taking on responsibility – whether as a class representative, in youth groups or in sports clubs. “I like looking after people, I like it when there's a good sense of community, and I admit that I also like being the boss,” the captain says with a grin. In May 2020, he demonstrated just that on the “Santos Express”. “We were on our way from Cartagena to Caucedo when our captain fell ill,” Cordes recounts. “He didn't have anything serious. But to play it safe, he had to go to the hospital. We had been joking around the whole voyage because I was in his office more than in mine as

jetzt 20 Minuten für die Übergabe – was willst du wissen?', dann war ich plötzlich erster Mann an Bord. Natürlich hatten wir alles kurzfristig mit unserem Flottenmanagement in Hamburg geklärt, dennoch war das eine echte Ausnahmesituation für mich." Für einen Moment wird Torben Cordes nachdenklich: „Da fährt dein Kapitän plötzlich im Krankenwagen mit Blaulicht davon und du kannst niemanden mehr fragen, was als Nächstes zu tun ist." Die Überfahrt nach Rotterdam funktionierte reibungslos, auch weil alle an Bord zusammenhielten, glaubt Torben Cordes. „Bei diesem Kapitän gab's samstags immer Waffeln und Kaffee auf der Brücke, das haben wir beibehalten und die ganze Besatzung dazu eingeladen. Und als er Fotos aus dem Krankenhaus schickte, habe ich natürlich die Crew informiert, dass es ihm gut gehen würde. Die Beförderung folgte nach der Reise auf der „Santos Express".

Es geht nur gemeinsam und wenn alle an einem Strang ziehen

Starkwinde und Schneemannsglück, Schwitzattacken und ein Cocktailabend

Gerade mal zwei Tage Kapitän in Kanada, schon kam die Meldung von Starkwinden in Tacoma. „Mit ordentlich Seitenwind aus dem Sund rauszufahren ist nicht ohne, da war ich schon aufgeregt. Als mich der Lotse fragt, seit wann ich Kapitän sei, war ich ehrlich – er hat mich dann besonders sorgfältig begleitet. Dann schipperten wir 300 Seemeilen mit der „Sofia Express" hoch bis nach Prince Rupert, wo uns der Wind richtig erwischte", berichtet der Kapitän: „Wir haben die folgenden fünf Monate trotz schlechten Wetters und

a result of my curiosity. Then, just before Santo Domingo, we sat together and he said: 'Torben, we now have 20 minutes for the handover. So what do you want to know?' Then I was suddenly the top man on board. Of course, we had clarified everything with our Fleet Management in Hamburg at short notice, but it was still a truly exceptional situation for me." However, the exhilaration was also mixed with a tinge of nervousness, he adds, saying: "There's your captain suddenly driving away in an ambulance with blue lights, and you can't ask anyone what to do next."

The crossing to Rotterdam went smoothly, which Cordes partly credits to the fact that everyone on board stuck together. "With this captain, we always had waffles and coffee on the bridge on Saturdays, so we kept that up and invited the whole crew to join us," he says. "And when he sent photos from the hospital, I naturally informed the crew that he would be fine."

The challenges – and joys – of being the captain

After the voyage on the "Santos Express" was completed, Cordes earned his promotion to captain. Just two days into his new role, word arrived in Vancouver of high winds to the south in Tacoma. "Sailing out of Puget Sound with a good crosswind is not without its problems, so I was already excited. When the pilot asked me how long I had been a captain, I was honest, so then he took extra care to guide me. Then we sailed 300 nautical miles on the 'Sofia Express' up to Prince Rupert, where the wind really caught us," the captain reports, adding: "We managed the following five months very well despite bad weather and many waiting times."

Closely interacting with others on board

Glücklich, wenn andere es auch sind: Torben Cordes findet es wichtig, sich immer wieder was Schönes für die Crew auszudenken

Happy when others are too: Cordes thinks it's important to always come up with something nice for the crew

>>

vieler Wartezeiten bestens gemeistert.“ Gemeinsam etwas an Bord zu unternehmen, auch mal zu fragen, ‚Hey, wie geht es

dir‘, egal ob den Oiler oder den Zweiten Offizier, das gehört für Torben Cordes dazu. „Wenn jemand traurig ist, will ich wissen warum – einfach um zu schauen, was ich tun kann.“ So war ein Wiper an Bord, dessen Vertrag wegen Corona zum fünften Mal verlängert werden musste. „Der ist bei mir im Büro in Tränen ausgebrochen, was ich verstehen konnte. Aber ich konnte ihn auch trösten und Mut machen. Und als wir Weihnachten vor Busan feierten, Spiele spielten und oben auf der Nock mit Schneemann und Weihnachtsmützen Fotos machten, lächelte auch der Wiper wieder – das sind für mich ganz wichtige Momente.“

Ausgleich findet der wasserbegeisterte Kapitän beim Windsurfen

The water-loving captain finds balance with windsurfing

Auch auf einer Reise mit der „Berlin Express“ letztes Jahr wusste er, wie er die strapazierte Mannschaft wieder motiviert: „Nach zwei Wochen Werftzeit in Dubai bei brütender Hitze, unendlich viel Arbeit und so gut wie keinem Tag, an dem man mal entspannen konnte, habe ich kurzerhand beschlossen, einen Cocktailabend als kleines Dankeschön zu organisieren. Wir besorgten Lebensmittelfarben und ein bisschen Deko und haben dann den farblich passenden Cocktail ‚Flag Of The Philippines‘ erfunden, natürlich alkoholfrei, speziell für unsere Wachgänger. Einfach mal an einem Sonntag auf See zusammensitzen und Zeit verbringen – das hat die Leute wieder motiviert! Es geht nur gemeinsam und wenn alle an einem Strang ziehen und glücklich sind“, findet der leidenschaftliche Seefahrer.

is very important to Cordes, even if it's just asking the oiler or the second officer how they are. “If someone is feeling down, I want to know why – just to see what I can do,” he says. As an example, he mentions a wiper on board whose contract had to be renewed for the fifth time owing to coronavirus-related restrictions on making crew changes. “He burst into tears in my office, which I could understand,” Cordes recounts. “But I could also comfort and encourage him. And when we celebrated Christmas before arriving in Busan, playing games and taking photos on top of the bridge wing with snowman and Christmas hats, the wiper also smiled again. These are very important moments for me.”

While sailing on the “Berlin Express” last year, he also knew how to motivate the strained crew again. “After two weeks of shipyard work in Dubai in sweltering heat, with an endless amount of work and virtually no days off to relax, I decided without further ado to organise a cocktail evening as a small thank-you,” he says. “We got food colouring and a little decoration and then invented the matching cocktail ‘Flag of the Philippines’ – of course alcohol-free, especially for our watch standers. Just sitting and spending time together on a Sunday at sea – that motivated people again! It only works together and when everyone pulls together and is happy.”

Happiness with family, surfboards and homecoming rituals

And what makes him happy in his private life? Of course, he could now mention the fantastic mountain bike trips in San Francisco or the breakfast on the beach in San Antonio, south of Valparaíso, that he treated himself to with a friend from work. “But you might not want to tell the trainees about that today, as they haven't

Glück mit Familie, Surfbrett und Brötchen

Und was macht ihn persönlich glücklich? Natürlich könnte er jetzt die fantastischen Ausflüge mit dem Mountainbike in San Francisco erwähnen, oder das Frühstück am Strand in San Antonio südlich von Valparaiso, das er sich mit einem befreundeten Kollegen gönnte. „Aber das mag man den Auszubildenden heute gar nicht erzählen – die durften coronabedingt bisher nicht einmal von Bord. Ich hoffe sehr, dass sich das bald ändert", so der Kapitän. Glück bedeutet für Torben Cordes auch das Nachhausekommen: „Wenn das letzte Stück der Heimreise ansteht und ich mit unserem Schiff bei Brunsbüttel auf der Elbe fahre, winken vom Ufer meine Eltern, in Stade kann ich mein Patenkind mit der Hupe begrüßen und sobald wir am Alten Land vorbeifahren, sehe ich als Erstes meine Frau am Lühe Anleger winkend mit ein paar Freunden oder Nachbarn stehen und kann unser Zuhause sehen. Sogar die Großeltern meiner Frau kriegen in Neu Wulmstorf mit, dass ich wieder da bin. Ein schöneres Begrüßungskomitee kann ich mir nicht vorstellen!", freut sich der Kapitän. Im Alten Land, wo er mit seiner Frau wohnt, relaxt er in seiner freien Zeit beim Heimwerken mit Holz oder verbringt Zeit mit Familie und Freunden. Und wann immer es möglich ist, geht's zum Windsurfen. „Sobald ich auf dem Brett stehe, kann ich komplett abschalten!" Gibt es ein Ritual, wenn er nach Hause kommt? „Als Erstes esse ich immer ein Rosinenbrötchen mit Zwiebelmett – sehr lecker! Das sollte jeder mal probieren."

even been allowed off the ship yet due to the coronavirus," the captain says, adding: "I really hope that will change soon."

For Cordes, happiness also means coming home. "When I'm on the last leg of the voyage home and I'm sailing our ship on the Elbe near Brunsbüttel, my parents wave from the shore. In Stade, I can greet my godchild with the horn. And once we pass Altes Land, the first thing I see is my wife standing at the Lühe jetty waving with a few friends or neighbours, and I can see our home. Even my wife's grandparents in Neu-Wulmsdorf realise that I'm back. I can't imagine a nicer welcoming committee!" the captain joyfully says.

Cordes lives with his wife in Altes Land, a big fruit-producing region downriver from Hamburg on the southwestern side of the Elbe. In his free time, he relaxes by doing DIY projects with wood or spending time with family and friends. And whenever possible, it's off to windsurf. "As soon as I'm on the board, I can completely switch off!" he says. When asked if he has a ritual whenever he arrives home, he says: "The first thing I always eat is a raisin roll with onion schmaltz. Very tasty! Everyone should try it!"

Was macht Torben Cordes heute?

Im Sommer reiste er mit seiner Frau im VW-Bulli durch Norwegen. „Wir kletterten zum ersten Mal auf den Preikestolen, gar nicht so einfach für uns Küstenkinder!", erzählt Torben Cordes. Der Preikestolen ist eine Felsplattform mit weitem Blick über den Lysefjord und angrenzende Berge. Mitte/Ende Oktober ist Cordes' nächster Einsatz auf der „Berlin Express" geplant. Die Route führt dann wieder durchs Mittelmeer und das Rote Meer in den Persischen Golf nach Pakistan, Indien und zurück.

What's Torben Cordes doing today?

In the summer, he and his wife travelled through Norway in a VW van. "We climbed Preikestolen for the first time – not so easy for us coastal kids!" Cordes says. Preikestolen, or Pulpit Rock, is steep cliff offering an expansive view over the Lysefjord and nearby mountains from the top. Cordes' next deployment, on the "Berlin Express", is schedule for mid-/late October. The route will take him through the Mediterranean and the Red Sea to the Persian Gulf, Pakistan and India – and then back again.

AL BAHIA

„Am meisten lernst du, wenn was schiefgeht“

Thorsten Schwarz

“You learn the most when something goes wrong”

Thorsten Schwarz hat auf seiner ersten Fahrt als Kapitän gleich zwei Stürme im Nordatlantik gemeistert. Hier erzählt er, wie man von einem Kurort in die weite Welt kommt, warum es lehrreich sein kann auf Grund zu laufen und welche Rolle eine Donauprinzessin für seine Berufswahl spielte.

During his very first voyage as a captain for Hapag-Lloyd, Thorsten Schwarz weathered two storms on the North Atlantic. Here, he discusses how to get from a small spa town to the wider world, why it can be instructive to run aground, and the role that a “Danube princess” played in his career choice.

Relaxen im Flensburger Museumshafen: Der gelernte Schiffsmechaniker könnte bei jeder Reparatur der betagten Schiffe behilflich sein

Relaxing in Flensburg's maritime museum: The trained ship mechanic could help with any needed repairs on the vintage ships

<<

Handwerker, Mediziner, Feuerwehrmann, Müllmanager, Unternehmer, Psychologe – als Kapitän hast du viele Berufe", erzählt Thorsten Schwarz: „Und genau das ist es, was mir so viel Spaß macht!" Bereits als Sechsjähriger beschloss er auf Borkum mit Blick auf einen alten Schlepper, Kapitän zu werden. „Das erzählen meine Eltern jedenfalls. Später habe ich dann mit Begeisterung ‚Die Donauprinzessin', eine TV-Serie rund um ein Flusskreuzfahrtschiff geguckt. Die Offiziere, die da herumliefen, die Atmosphäre, das hat mich fasziniert. Und tatsächlich haben wir mal eine Fahrt auf der echten ‚Donauprinzessin' gemacht, wo mir der Kapitän die Brücke gezeigt und alles erklärt hat." Von da war es nicht weit zum Infostand des Verbands Deutscher Reeder: „Das war auf einer Ausbildungsmesse. Der Mann dort nahm sich Zeit für mich, ich habe ihn bestimmt zwei Stunden mit meinen Fragen gelöchert!"

A captain wears a lot of hats – craftsman, doctor, fireman, waste manager, entrepreneur, psychologist," says Thorsten Schwarz. "And that's exactly what is so much fun about it!" While looking at an old tugboat as a 6-year-old on the North Sea island of Borkum, Schwarz decided he wanted to become a captain. "Or at least that's what my parents like to tell people," he admits. "Later, I was a huge fan of 'The Danube Princess', a TV series about a river cruise ship. I was fascinated by all the officers running around and the atmosphere. And, in fact, we actually did take a voyage on the real 'Danube Princess' once, and the captain showed me the bridge and explained to me how everything works."

From a small city to a zoo in Jordan

From there, it wasn't far to the information

Von der Kleinstadt in den Zoo von Jordanien

Es folgte ein Praktikum auf der alten „Frankfurt Express" – die erste Begegnung mit Hapag-Lloyd. „Eine unvergessliche Reise", schwärmt der 35-Jährige: „Ich komme aus Bad Salzuflen, einem kleinen Kurort in der Nähe vom Teutoburger Wald. Wenn du als 16-Jähriger in Singapur und Kuala Lumpur an Land darfst, in Jordanien den Zoo besuchst oder in Djakarta auf Sightseeingtour gehst, das ist überwältigend. Auch die Arbeit an Bord hat mich begeistert. Wir durften überall mitmachen, vom Steuern des Schiffes bis zum Auseinandernehmen der Maschine – einfach klasse!" Seine Eltern hatten gehofft, er sei nach dem Praktikum kuriert, aber Thorsten Schwarz wollte sofort die Schule schmeißen und bei Hapag-Lloyd anfangen – nicht mit Klaus Heinig, dem damaligen Personalleiter: „Ich sehe Sie in drei Jahren! Machen Sie erst mal die Schule zu Ende!" Nach dem Abitur konnte sich Thorsten Schwarz endlich bei Hapag-Lloyd bewerben – Startschuss für eine Karriere, die 2020 zur Erfüllung seines Kindheitstraumes führte.

Wenn es plötzlich ruhig wird und alles rot blinkt

In den 16 Jahren bis zum Kapitänspatent lernte Thorsten Schwarz die Seefahrt von der Pike auf kennen. Als Schiffsmechaniker fuhr er den damaligen Sammelservice von Europa, über Nordamerika bis Asien und wieder zurück, dann als nautischer Wachoffizier und schließlich fünf Jahre als Erster Offizier. „Am meisten lernst du, wenn was schiefgeht", so Schwarz und berichtet von einem Vorfall, der sich noch vor seinem Studium ereignete: „Das war 2008 auf der alten ‚Norfolk Express', als ich noch Schiffsmechaniker war. Ich wachte mitten in der Nacht auf, weil es plötzlich ganz ruhig wurde. In meiner

stand of the German Shipowners' Association (VDR). "That was at a trade fair for apprenticeships. The man there spent a lot of time with me, and I must have peppered him with questions for two whole hours!" This was followed by an internship on the old "Frankfurt Express", which was Schwarz's first encounter with Hapag-Lloyd. "It was an unforgettable voyage," the 35-year-old fondly recalls. "I come from Bad Salzuflen, a small spa town near the Teutoburg Forest. But when you get to go ashore as a 16-year-old in Singapore and Kuala Lumpur, to visit the zoo in Jordan, or to go sightseeing in Jakarta, it's simply mind-blowing. And I also really liked the work on board. We were allowed to help out with everything, from steering the ship to taking the engine apart. It was just fantastic!"

As long as the captain doesn't get nervous, everything will be just fine

Schwarz's parents had hoped he would be cured of his new fascination after the internship. But he actually wanted to drop out of school immediately and start working for Hapag-Lloyd. Klaus Heinig, the Head of HR at the time, didn't let this happen, though, telling Schwarz instead: "I'll see you in three years! But first go and finish school!" After graduating from high school, Schwarz was finally able to apply for a job at Hapag-Lloyd – in what was the start of a career that would eventually lead, in 2020, to the fulfilment of his childhood dream.

When things suddenly grow silent and everything is blinking red

In the 16 years it took him to earn his master's license, Schwarz learned the art of seafaring from the bottom up. As a

Kammer hatte ich ein eigenes Alarmtableau, auf dem alles rot blinkte. Da dachte ich: „Okay, ich geh jetzt mal runter." Der Chefingenieur wartete schon , sagte nur: „Thorsten, gut, dass du da bist, wir sind auf Grund gelaufen." Ich konnte es zunächst gar nicht glauben, dachte, dass er Spaß macht. Aber es war tatsächlich passiert. Zwei Wochen lang lagen wir oberhalb des Suezkanals fest, bevor wir freikamen. In den ersten Tagen versuchten Schlepper uns freizuziehen, leider mit schwachem Erfolg. Dann kam eine Bunkerbarge, die circa 2.000 Tonnen unseres Schweröls abpumpte, was weitere vier Tage dauerte – schließlich versuchten wir, mit unserer eigenen Maschine stoßweise freizukommen. Das funktionierte! Danach untersuchten Taucher die Außenhülle – sie war glücklicherweise nur eingedrückt."

Solange der Kapitän nicht nervös wird, ist alles in Ordnung

Eigentlich sollte die Reise drei Monate dauern, aber die Reederei bat Thorsten Schwarz mit in die Werft zu fahren. „Also machten wir uns auf den Weg nach Singapur. Und gerieten im Indischen Ozean prompt in einen Sturm. Drei Tage lang nur mit Rettungsweste, kaum jemand schlief. Alles flog durch die Gegend. Sogar die schweren Holztische in den Kammern wanderten hin und her. Es gab den einen oder anderen Moment, wo ich dachte, jetzt kippt das Schiff", berichtet Kapitän Schwarz. „Alle haben aufeinander aufgepasst, die Besatzung wächst durch so was unglaublich gut zusammen. Und Kapitän Bultmann war der ruhende Pol, ich dachte nur, solange der Kapitän nicht nervös wird, ist alles in Ordnung." Die dreieinhalb Wochen auf der Werft in Singapur waren für Thorsten Schwarz eine weitere Erfahrung: „Ganze Schotts

ship mechanic, he sailed on the then-collective service from Europe to Asia via North America and back again. Then he became an officer of the watch and then a chief officer five years later.

"You learn the most when something goes wrong," Schwarz says before recounting a story of an incident he experienced before his university studies. "That was in 2008, when I was a ship mechanic on the old 'Norfolk Express,'" he says. "I woke up in the middle of the night because it had suddenly become completely quiet. I had my own alarm panel in my cabin, and everything on it was flashing red. So I thought, 'OK, I'm going to go down to the engine room now.' The chief engineer was already waiting for me there, and he just said: 'Thorsten, it's good you're here. We've run aground.' I couldn't believe it, I thought he was joking. But it was actually true. We were stuck above the Suez Canal for two weeks before we managed to break free. In the first few days, tugboats tried to pull us free, but unfortunately with little success. Then a bunker barge came and pumped out about 2,000 tonnes of our heavy fuel oil, which took another four days. Finally, we tried to jerk ourselves free by repeatedly gunning our engine. And it worked! Then the divers checked the outer hull for damage, but luckily it had only been dented."

The voyage was actually supposed to last three months, but the shipping company asked Schwarz to accompany the ship into dry dock. "So we set off for Singapore – and promptly found ourselves in a storm on the Indian Ocean. We had to keep our life jackets on for three days straight, and hardly anyone got any sleep. Things were flying all over the place. Even the heavy wooden tables in the cabins were sliding back and forth.

Wie man sich als Kapitän fit hält? Thorsten Schwarz schwört auf EMS-Training: „Höllisch anstrengend, aber sehr effektiv!"

How does a captain stay fit? Schwarz swears by EMS training: "Exhausting as hell, but very effective!"

>>

Begeisterter Kapitän und Bäcker: In seiner freien Zeit backt Thorsten Schwarz gern, seine Spezialität ist Maulwurftorte

Avld captain and baker: Schwarz likes to bake in his free time. His specialty: mole cake

wurden rausgebrannt, die Außenhülle an den eingedrückten Stellen ausgetauscht. Die Werftarbeiter waren Tag und Nacht im Einsatz. Solche Reisen prägen sich ein. Da sammelst du Erfahrungen, die du nie wieder vergisst!"

Abwettern im Bermuda Dreieck, Wissen teilen mit der Crew

Im November 2020 wurde Thorsten Schwarz zum Kapitän ernannt. Und seine erste Fahrt hielt gleich zwei Stürme für ihn bereit. „Nach meiner Beförderung ging es im Sommer letzten Jahres nach

In fact, there were one or two moments when I thought the ship was going to capsize," Captain Schwarz recalls. "Everybody looked out for everybody else, and a crew grows incredibly tight when they go through something like that together. Captain Bultmann was the calming influence. And I just thought: 'As long as the captain doesn't get nervous, everything will be just fine.'"

Spending three and a half weeks in the shipyard in Singapore was another new experience for Schwarz. "Entire bulkheads were removed with cutting

Genua, wo ich auf die ‚Vienna Express' einstieg. Nach der Übergabe war ich ab Valencia allein verantwortlicher Kapitän – am Ziel meiner Träume! Kurz vor New York wartete der erste Sturm, der aber glimpflich verlief, weil wir ihn nördlich bei sieben Meter hohen Wellen umschifften, aber auf der zweiten Rundreise zog ein weit mächtigeres Sturmtief über den Atlantik. Im Hafen bleiben oder losfahren, nach Süden oder Norden? Das war jetzt meine Entscheidung. Ich entschied, Richtung Süden zu den Bermuda Islands zu fahren, um dort vier Tage abzuwettern – was genau richtig war." Und das, erklärt der Kapitän, sei das Großartige bei Hapag-Lloyd: „Du wirst als Kapitän nicht infrage gestellt, dein Wort gilt. Das gibt einem eine unglaubliche Sicherheit." Eines seiner größten Vorbilder? „Kapitän Peter Rößler", erzählt Thorsten Schwarz: „Seine Erfahrung, sein Durchsetzungsvermögen, aber auch die Fähigkeit, Wissen zu teilen – das habe ich mir von ihm abgeguckt", lächelt er verschmitzt und freut sich auf seinen nächsten Einsatz.

torches, and the dented parts of the outer shell were replaced. The shipyard staff was working around the clock. These kinds of voyages leave a lasting impression. You gain experiences that you never forget!"

Weathering the Bermuda Triangle, sharing knowledge with the crew

Schwarz was finally promoted to captain in November 2020, and his first voyage as a captain held two storms in store for him. "After I was promoted, I went to Genoa last summer, where I boarded the 'Vienna Express'. After the handover in Valencia, I had sole responsibility for the ship as its captain – meaning that I had finally made my dream come true! The first storm was waiting for us off New York, but it wasn't so bad because we sailed around it to the north in seven-metre waves. On the second round voyage, however, a far more powerful storm front passed over the Atlantic. We asked ourselves: 'Should we stay in port or cast off? And, if so, should we sail north or south?' That was now my decision to make. I then opted to head south to the Bermuda Islands to wait out the storm for four days – which was exactly the right thing to do." And that, the captain explains, is the great thing about Hapag-Lloyd. "Nobody really challenges your judgment as a captain, and you have the final say. And that trust gives you an incredible feeling of confidence."

When asked who his biggest role model has been, Schwarz says: "Captain Peter Rössler. His vast experience, his ability to assert himself, but also his ability to share knowledge – that's something I've picked up from him," he says with a mischievous smile, adding that he is looking forward to his next assignment.

Was macht Thorsten Schwarz heute?

Im Sommer 2022 arbeitete Thorsten Schwarz viele Schichten im Rettungsdienst und absolvierte eine Ausbildung zum Rettungssanitäter in Flensburg. Seine langjährige Tätigkeit beim Roten Kreuz hilft ihm auch an Bord. Aktuell fährt er auf der „Vienna Express" Richtung Asien.

What's Thorsten Schwarz doing today?

In summer 2022, Schwarz worked many shifts in the ambulance service and completed paramedic training in Flensburg. His many years of service with the Red Cross also come in handy on board. He is currently sailing to Asia on the "Vienna Express".

Elbaufwärts: Kapitän Jonathan Pompe mit der „Kyoto Express" auf dem Weg zum Container Terminal Altenwerder.

Upstream: Captain Janathan Pompe and the "Kyoto Express" on their way to Hamburg's Container Terminal Altenwerder

UASC
tex

EXPRESS

BEACON
TRITON
EXPRESS

VB RASANT

tex
ONE

KYOTO EXPRESS
HAMBURG
IMO 9295256
AIRBUS

„Meine Heimat ist die Welt“

Silke Muschitz

“The world is my home”

Silke Muschitz ist nicht nur Kapitänin, sondern auch leitende Direktorin für das zur See fahrende Personal bei Hapag-Lloyd. In dieser Funktion kümmert sie sich seit April 2020 um 1.300 Seeleute weltweit. Als erste Frau in rund 600 Jahren Bestehen wurde sie Mitglied in der Lübecker Schifffahrtsgesellschaft, die Zeitschrift Capital wählte sie 2021 unter die wichtigsten „40 unter 40“ der jungen Wirtschaftselite. Angefangen hat diese fulminante Karriere mit einem Kinderlexikon.

Silke Muschitz is not only a captain, but also Senior Director Marine Human Resources at Hapag-Lloyd. In this role, she has been looking after 1,300 seafarers worldwide since April 2020. She was the first woman ever admitted to the Schifffahrtsgesellschaft in the over-600-year history of this Lübeck-based shipowners guild, and she was voted one of the "Top 40 under 40" up-and-coming talents shaping Germany by the business magazine Capital in 2021. This dazzling career all began with a children's encyclopaedia.

Auch wenn sie nicht mehr zur See fährt, Kapitänsmütze und die Uniform hängen griffbereit im Schrank

Even though she no longer sails, her captain's cap and uniform hang ready for use in her wardrobe

<<

Silke Muschitz hat das Buch mitgebracht, das bei ihr die große Sehnsucht weckte, ein Bilderlexikon, das Kindern die Welt erklärt. Sie schlägt die entscheidende Doppelseite auf: ein Kreuzfahrtschiff im Querschnitt, detailgetreu illustriert von der Brücke bis zur Schiffsschraube. „Wasser zog mich schon immer magisch an. Wenn ich mit meinen Eltern im Urlaub an der See war, beobachtete ich die Schiffe, wie sie hin- und herfuhren, fragte mich, was eigentlich dahintersteckt", erzählt die gebürtige Österreicherin. „Und dann hatte ich im Kindergarten dieses Buch, konnte mich gar nicht sattsehen an den vielen Einzelheiten des Schiffes. Später schenkten mir meine Eltern das Lexikon sogar zu Weihnachten", so die 35-Jährige. Mit 15 kam sie mit dem Vater einer Freundin ins Gespräch: „Er war Kapitän und erzählte mit großer Leidenschaft von seinem Beruf – da dachte ich spontan: Das will ich auch!"

Silke Muschitz brought along the book that sparked her intense interest: an encyclopaedia that explains the world to children using pictures. She opens the crucial two-page spread: a cross-section of a cruise ship, illustrated in detail from the bridge to the propeller. "Water has always had a magical pull on me. When I was on holiday at the seaside with my parents, I would watch the ships as they sailed back and forth, wondering what they were really all about," says the 35-year-old native of Austria. "And then I had this book in kindergarten and couldn't get enough of all the details about the ship. Later, my parents even gave me a copy of the encyclopaedia for Christmas!" When she was 15, Muschitz got into a conversation with the father of a friend. "He was a captain and talked about his job with great passion. And that's when I suddenly thought: 'I want to do that, too!'"

Die Welt hat Silke Muschitz bereits als Jugendliche gesehen. „Mein Vater war Diplomat. Ich verbrachte meine Kindheit in Jerusalem, in Österreich, die erste Schulzeit in Moskau, Peking und dann ging es nach Washington, wo ich später auch Abitur gemacht habe", berichtet sie. Abschied nehmen, immer wieder neue Kontakte knüpfen in den jeweiligen Ländern und Orten, sich öffnen für fremde Menschen und Kulturen, das habe sie dadurch gelernt. Nicht die schlechteste Voraussetzung, zur See zu fahren, oder wie Silke Muschitz es formuliert: „Meine Heimat ist die Welt."

Rost klopfen, malen, Kreuzfahrtgefühle

Ihre Ausbildung bei Hapag-Lloyd begann sie 2005, ihr Berufsberater hatte vergeblich versucht, sie davon abzubringen. „Ich kam aus dem Beratungsgespräch, dachte, jetzt erst recht – das war die beste Entscheidung. Ich kann nur allen jungen Leuten raten: Lasst euch nicht beirren, macht euer Ding!"

Mit der betagten „Frankfurt Express" begann ihre erste Reise von Hamburg durch den Suezkanal bis in den Golf von Thailand und wieder zurück. „Auch wenn man vier Wochen an Land auf den Einsatz vorbereitet wird, der durchgetaktete Arbeitsalltag, das Zusammenleben an Bord mit so vielen verschiedenen Menschen, auch die anfangs ungewohnte Hierarchie – das war eine vollkommen neue Welt für mich." Silke Muschitz war die einzige Frau unter neun Auszubildenden. „Aber an Bord ist es in der Regel völlig egal, ob du männlich, weiblich oder divers bist, entscheidend ist, dass du deinen Job erledigst. Wenn ein Rettungsboot zu Wasser gelassen werden muss, diskutierst du nicht, ob das ein Mann oder eine Frau anordnet, das muss einfach gemacht werden!" Rost klopfen und Malen gehörten

Muschitz had already seen the world in her youth. "My father was a diplomat," she says. I spent my early years in Jerusalem and Austria, my first school years in Moscow and Beijing, and then I went to Washington, where I later graduated from high school." How to say goodbye, how to always make new contacts in new countries and places, and how to be open to foreign people and cultures – those are some of the skills she learned along the way. Muschitz notes that this wasn't the worst preparation for going to sea, adding: "The world is my home."

I can only advise all young people: Don't be deterred! Just do your thing!

Knocking off rust, painting, cruise feelings

Muschitz started an apprenticeship at Hapag-Lloyd in 2005 even though her career counsellor had tried in vain to dissuade her. "I came out of the counselling session thinking that, now more than ever, this was the best decision," she says. "I can only advise all young people: Don't be deterred! Just do your thing!"

Her first voyage, on the ageing "Frankfurt Express", took her from Hamburg through the Suez Canal to the Gulf of Thailand and back again. "Even though you spend four weeks onshore preparing for the deployment, it was still completely new for me to have a well-scheduled working day and to live together on board with so many different people, not to mention the initially unfamiliar hierarchy," she says. Of nine apprentices, Muschitz was the only woman. "But, on board, it usually doesn't matter whether you are male, female or diverse. What matters is that you do your job," she

als Auszubildende zu ihren Hauptaufgaben, die alte „Frankfurt Express" bot dafür reichlich Gelegenheit. „Wenn ich heute darauf zurückblicke, bin ich froh über diese Erfahrung. Ich weiß, wie es sich anfühlt, wenn man den ganzen Tag einfach nur Metall bearbeitet. Später als Erste Offizierin habe ich darauf geachtet, dass die Leute nicht immer dasselbe machen, sondern auch leichtere bzw. andere Aufgaben zugeteilt bekommen."

Mein Rat für junge Leute: Lasst euch nicht beirren, macht euer Ding!

Fürs Studium zog die damals 21-jährige Silke Muschitz 2007 nach Bremen, später nach Lübeck, um dem Wasser noch näher zu sein, denn Segeln ist mittlerweile ihre zweite Leidenschaft. Es folgten zwei Jahre als Dritte und Zweite Offizierin, 2012 wurde sie zur Ersten Nautischen Offizierin befördert. Auf die Frage nach ihren Lieblingsgebieten gibt Silke Muschitz lachend zu, dass sie lieber bei warmen Temperaturen über die Meere schippert. „Einmal musste ich in Halifax (Kanada) sechs Stunden Ladungswache bei bis zu minus 20 Grad gehen – ich war noch Tage später nicht wieder aufgetaut. Singapur bei 40 Grad ist dagegen super, ich bin sehr gern die Nordeuropa-Asien-Route gefahren, später als Kapitänin dann mit der ‚Chicago Express' vom Mittelmeer zur Ostküste der USA: Algeciras, Südfrankreich, Italien, New York, Norfolk, Savannah, Miami – das war schon fast wie eine Kreuzfahrt."

Der kleine Unterschied, der große Sprung

Dass einer Frau an Bord der Wind manchmal doch etwas anders um die Nase weht, erlebte sie als Erste Offizierin in Asien. „Ich war mit einem sehr erfahrenen

notes. "If a lifeboat has to be launched, you don't discuss whether a man or a woman gave the order. It just has to get done!" Knocking off rust and painting were among her main tasks as an apprentice, and the old "Frankfurt Express" offered plenty of opportunity for this. "When I look back on it today, I'm glad that I had this experience," she says. "I know how it feels to just work on metal all day long. Later, as chief mate, I made sure that people didn't always do the same thing, but were also assigned easier or different tasks."

In 2007, when she was 21 years old, Muschitz moved to Bremen for her studies, but she later moved to Lübeck to be even closer to the water, as sailing had become her second passion. After spending two years as a third and second officer, she was promoted to chief mate in 2012. When asked about her favourite places to work, Muschitz laughingly admits that she prefers to sail in warmer climates. "I once had to stand cargo watch for six hours in Halifax [Canada] at temperatures as low as minus 20 degrees. Days later, I still hadn't thawed out yet," she recounts. "On the other hand, Singapore at 40 degrees is super, and I really liked to sail the North Europe-Asia route and then later, after becoming a captain, the route from the Mediterranean to the US East Coast on the 'Chicago Express'. Algeciras, southern France, Italy, New York, Norfolk, Savannah, Miami – it was almost like a cruise."

The small difference, the big leap

As a chief officer in Asia, she found out that the wind sometimes blows a bit differently for a woman on board. "I was with a very experienced captain and a very good chief engineer on the 'Prague

Mitten im Hamburger Hafen: Silke Muschitz, die Elbphilharmonie und das Museumsschiff „Cap San Diego"

In the middle of the Port of Hamburg: Muschitz, the Elbphilharmonie concert hall and the "Cap San Diego" museum ship

>>

Mehr Frauen an Bord und in den Führungsetagen? Aber immer! Silke Muschitz geht mit gutem Beispiel voran

More women on board and in leadership positions? Absolutely! Muschitz is setting a good example

Kapitän und einem sehr guten Leitenden Ingenieur auf der ‚Prague Express', die Hapag-Lloyd verchartert hatte. Der zuständige Hafenplaner kam an Bord und ich spürte an seiner Art sofort, dass ihm eine Frau an Deck nicht so recht passte, und schon gar nicht eine, die anderer Meinung ist. Ich erklärte ihm, dass er seine Container anders platzieren müsse, weil an der gewünschten Stelle ein Freifallboot steht. Es dauerte ewig, bis ich mich durchgesetzt hatte, aber am Ende hatte ich die besseren Argumente. Der Kapitän griff nicht ein, hörte aber von nebenan zu und sagte hinterher: ‚Das musst du später auch allein können.' Und damit hatte er recht." Kommunikation an Bord sei ohnehin eine besondere Sache: „Die Mentalitäten können sehr verschieden sein, da braucht es Einfühlungsvermögen. Mit Deutschen redet man anders als mit Filipinos, das lernt man mit der Zeit." Silke Muschitz findet es wichtig, dass nicht zu viele unterschiedliche Nationalitäten an Bord sind. Die Crew bestehe in der Regel aus Europäern und Filipinos: „Das passt sehr gut", erzählt sie.

Wie sie den Aufstieg von der Ersten Offizierin zur Kapitänin geschafft hat? „Nach ein paar Jahren Berufserfahrung stellte sich eine gewisse Routine ein und ich hatte Zeit, zu beobachten, was der Kapitän so macht. Du fragst dich, was würde ich jetzt tun und merkst mit der Zeit, ich glaube, ich kann das jetzt." Wichtig sei es, so die heutige Personalchefin, dass man auch der Reederei ein Signal gebe: „Als ich mich fit genug fühlte, bat ich meinen Vorgänger Arnold Lipinski um ein Gespräch. Und er sagte nur ‚Gut, dann

Express', which Hapag-Lloyd had chartered out," Muschitz recounts. "The port planner in charge came on board, and I immediately sensed from his demeanour that a woman on deck wasn't really to his liking – and especially one that doesn't agree with him. I explained to him that he had to place his containers differently because there was a free-fall lifeboat at the desired location. It took me forever to get my way, but I ultimately had the better arguments. Rather than getting involved, the captain merely listened in from the next room and afterwards said: 'Later on, you'll have to be able to do that on your own, too.' And he was right about that." In any case, communication on board is a special thing. "People's mindsets can be very different, so you need to have a lot of empathy," Muschitz says. "Over time, you learn that you speak differently with Germans than with Filipinos." Muschitz thinks it's important to not have too many different nationalities on board. The crew is usually made up of Europeans and Filipinos, she says, adding that this is "a very good fit".

In response to a question about how she managed to make it from chief mate to captain, Muschitz says: "A certain routine set in after a few years of work experience, and I had time to observe what the captain was doing. You ask yourself, 'What would I do now?' And, over time, you realise, 'I think I can do this now.'" Muschitz, who now works as Senior Director Marine Human Resources, also thinks it's important to give signals to the shipping company. "When I felt up to it, I asked my predecessor, Arnold Lipinski, for a talk," she says. "And he just said, 'Well, let's take a look at that now.'" Two years later, the time had come. Muschitz became the youngest of 89 captains and one of three female captains at Hapag-Lloyd at that time. "When I put the epaulettes

gucken wir uns das jetzt mal an.‘ Zwei Jahre später war es so weit. Silke Muschitz wurde die jüngste von 89 Kapitänen und eine von damals drei Kapitäninnen bei Hapag-Lloyd: „Als ich mir in Genua nach dem Overlapping zum ersten Mal die Epauletten auf die Schulter schob, dachte ich: ‚Jetzt gibt es kein Zurück mehr!‘“ Und in diesem Fall stimmte das wortwörtlich, denn ihre erste Reise mit der „Chicago Express“ führte die frisch beförderte Kapitänin nicht auf Hin- und Rückfahrt, sondern rund um den Globus: „Wir fuhren Richtung Suezkanal, als wir die Information bekamen, den Dienst zu wechseln. Jetzt sollten wir nach Asien, dann weiter über den Pazifik und dann durch den Panamakanal fahren. Ich dachte nur, Pazifik? Im Winter? Wer einmal zu dieser Jahreszeit über den Nordpazifik gefahren ist, weiß was für Stürme einen da erwarten können. Ich fand die Herausforderung, mit 37-köpfiger Besatzung inklusive unserer Auszubildenden zu fahren, schon genug. Dann verließen wir in Shanghai den Hafen und das Wetter war von den Aleuten bis Hawaii einfach nur schlecht. Nördlich oder südlich von Japan fahren? Abwettern oder durchfahren? Die Entscheidung, welcher Kurs der richtige ist, nimmt dir keiner ab. Alle sechs Stunden änderte sich die Wetterlage. Nach der Küstenreise in den USA und zurück in Panama stieg ich ins Flugzeug nach Hamburg, somit war es eine komplette Weltumrundung.“

Zwischen Meeresrauschen und Pandemie

Sobald Silke Muschitz über die Faszination der Seefahrt spricht, funkeln ihre grünen Augen: „Dieser Moment, wenn du komplett vom Meer umgeben bist, dein Blick ins Unendliche schweift, ihn nichts begrenzt. Dazu der Mix aus frischer Luft und dem Geruch des Schiffes, das

on my shoulder for the first time in Genoa after the overlapping, I thought: ‘There’s no turning back now!’” And that was literally true in this case, as her first voyage on the training vessel the “Chicago Express” took the newly promoted captain not on a round voyage, but around the globe. “We were heading towards the Suez Canal when we got the information to switch services,” Muschitz recounts. “Now we were supposed to go to Asia, then on across the Pacific and then through the Panama Canal. I just thought: ‘The Pacific? In winter?’ Anyone who has sailed across the North Pacific at this time of year knows what kinds of storms you can expect there. I already found the challenge of sailing with a crew of 37, including our apprentices, enough. Then we left port in Shanghai, and the weather was nothing but awful from the Aleutian Islands to Hawaii. Should we sail north or south of Japan? Should we wait for the storm to pass by or just sail through it? The decision about which course is the right one is yours and yours alone to make. The weather was changing every six hours. Once we were back in Panama after making calls on the US West Coast, I got on a plane to Hamburg, so it was a complete round-the-world voyage.”

I know how it feels to just work on metal all day long

Between the sounds of the sea and the pandemic

Muschitz’s green eyes light up as soon as she talks about her fascination with seafaring. “That moment when you are completely surrounded by the sea, when you’re gazing out into an infinity without limits. Add to that the mix of fresh air and the smell of the ship, the pounding of the

Stampfen der Maschine und das Meeresrauschen, da fällt der ganze Alltag von dir ab und du denkst einfach nur noch, wie schön diese Welt ist – das ist mit nichts zu vergleichen", schwärmt sie. Dennoch tauschte sie 2020 die Brücke mit dem Büro am Ballindamm. „Ich war sehr glücklich an Bord – aber ich hatte auch eine leise Ahnung, dass da noch mehr ist, was mich interessiert." 2019 fragte Personalchef Arnold Lipinski, ob sie sich vorstellen können, seine Nachfolgerin zu werden. „Ich habe spontan Ja gesagt – an den Rest des Gesprächs kann ich mich nicht mehr erinnern", lacht sie. Es folgte ein weiterer Einsatz über Weihnachten und Silvester auf der „Chicago Express". „Im Februar 2020 fand das obligatorische Reisegespräch statt, dachte ich jedenfalls, da sagte Arnold Lipinski: ‚Nächsten Monat können Sie hier anfangen.' Ich fiel aus allen Wolken! Dann kam Corona."

Mit Transparenz und Ehrlichkeit kamen wir durch die Pandemie

Silke Muschitz erlebte den Wechsel in die Personalabteilung mit allen Unwägbarkeiten, die die Pandemie mit sich brachte. „Die Leute konnten teilweise monatelang nicht von Bord, die Angst vor Corona war riesig, es gab noch keinen Impfstoff. Und ich saß plötzlich im Homeoffice, ohne große Ahnung von Outlook und PowerPoint. Bei meiner ersten Online-Sitzung wusste ich nicht mal, wo ich klicken sollte, um teilzunehmen. Wenn ich daran zurückdenke, muss ich über mich selbst lachen." Aber dann habe sie einfach gemacht: „Das Auswärtige Amt kontaktieren, mit den Botschaften verhandeln, der ganze Papierkram – das war das eine. Den Crews Hoffnung und Zuversicht geben, war aber noch viel wichtiger. Wir standen in sehr engem Kontakt mit

engine and the sound of the sea, and all of your everyday life falls away and you just think how beautiful this world is – nothing can compare to that," she nostalgically notes. Nevertheless, Muschitz switched from a ship's bridge to an office on the Ballindamm in 2020. "I was very happy on board, but I also had a faint sense that there was something more that I was interested in," she says. In 2019, Arnold Lipinski asked Muschitz if she could imagine filling his shoes as Head of Marine HR. "I immediately said 'Yes!' – though I can't remember the rest of the conversation," she says with a laugh. This was followed by another deployment over Christmas and New Year's Eve on the "Chicago Express". "In February 2020, I was going to have the mandatory voyage talk, or so I thought, when Arnold Lipinski said: 'Next month, you can start here.' I was completely flabbergasted! And then the coronavirus arrived."

Muschitz experienced the switch to the HR department with all the uncertainties that came along with the pandemic. "Some people couldn't get off their ships for months, there was huge fear of the coronavirus, and there weren't any vaccines yet. And suddenly I was sitting in my home office, not knowing much about how to use Outlook or PowerPoint. During my first online meeting, I didn't even know which button to click to join in. When I think back on it, I have to laugh at myself," she says with a grin. But then she simply did it, saying: "Contacting Germany's Foreign Office, negotiating with embassies, all the paperwork – that was one thing. But giving the crews hope and reassurance was even more important. We kept in very close contact with our captains and the ports, and we sent out regular newsletters with all the info. Plus, we had to look

Ihre Sehnsucht nach Weite und Wasser stillt die Flottenchefin heute beim Segeln auf der Ostsee

Today, the Head of Fleet Management satisfies her longing for open spaces and water by sailing on the Baltic Sea

>>

Stolz mit Wahrzeichen: Die Flottenchefin an den Landungsbrücken vor dem legendären Großsegler „Rickmer Rickmers"

Distinguished and proud: The Head of Fleet Management at Hamburg's Landungsbrücken jetty in front of the legendary tall ship the "Rickmer Rickmers"

unseren Kapitänen und den Häfen, verschickten regelmäßig Newsletter mit allen Infos. Und an Bord mussten wir schauen, wie man eine Person, die sich infiziert hat, separieren kann, ohne dass sie sich komplett ausgeschlossen fühlt. Oder wie man Essenszeiten taktet, um die Begegnungen zu reduzieren, welche Hygienemaßnahmen zusätzlich getroffen werden können. Glücklicherweise hatten wir keine schweren Verläufe. Die Personalführung aus der Distanz war neu für mich, aber unglaublich spannend, weil ich gelernt habe, was gute Kommunikation

into things on board – like how to separate a person who has become infected without making them feel completely excluded, how to schedule mealtimes to minimise encounters, and which additional hygiene measures needed to be implemented. Luckily, we didn't have any severe cases. Managing staff from a distance was something new for me, but also incredibly exciting, as it taught me what good communication can do – that transparency and honesty build trust. And that's how we got through the pandemic in good shape." Muschitz says that the lockdowns in Asia

leisten kann: Transparenz und Ehrlichkeit schaffen Vertrauen. So sind wir gut durch die Pandemie gekommen.“ Die Lockdowns in Asien seien zwar auch jetzt noch herausfordernd, aber insgesamt lockere sich alles, freut sich Silke Muschitz. „Das spiegelt sich auch in den Reisegesprächen mit den Kapitänen. Wir reden über die Reise, ob sie gut oder eher schwierig war, über die Stimmung an Bord, und wenn es nicht ganz rundlief, ändern wir die Konstellationen. Oder wenn es in einer Familie einen Trauerfall gab, dann weiß ich, diesen Kapitän frage ich in nächster Zeit auf keinen Fall, ob er notfallmäßig einspringen kann.“ Die Reisegespräche dienten auch dafür, Prozesse zu optimieren oder zu schauen, ob sich bestimmte Unfälle häufen und wie gegebenenfalls gegengesteuert werden könne. „Andererseits erzähle ich unseren Kapitänen auch, was bei Hapag-Lloyd an Land gerade so los ist, was wir tun, ob wir neue Schiffe ordern, welche Technik wir probieren. So fühlen sich alle miteinander verbunden. Ich glaube, das ist die große Stärke von Hapag-Lloyd.“ Silke Muschitz’ Stärke ist weit mehr als fachliches Wissen und Führungskompetenz, sie ist von Kopf bis Fuß leidenschaftliche Seefahrerin: „Auch wenn ich jetzt an Land vor dem Computer sitze, kann ich zu jedem und jeder unserer Seeleute sagen: ‚Ich weiß, wie du dich fühlst!‘“

are still presenting challenges, but happily adds that everything is easing on the whole. “This is also reflected in the voyage talks with the captains,” she continues. We talk about the voyage, whether it was good or rather difficult, and about the mood on board. And if anything didn’t go quite right, we change the configurations. Or if there’s been a death in a family, I know there’s no way I’m asking that captain to step in on an emergency basis anytime soon.” The voyage talks are also used to optimise processes and to see whether certain accidents are occurring more frequently and, if so, how to take any needed countermeasures. “On the other hand, I also tell our captains what’s going on at Hapag-Lloyd on shore, what we are doing, whether we are ordering new ships, and which technologies we are trying out,” she explains. “This makes everybody feel connected. And I think that this is Hapag-Lloyd’s greatest strength.” Muschitz’s strength is far more than technical knowledge and leadership skills, as she is a passionate seafarer from head to toe. “Even though I’m sitting in front of the computer on land now, I can say to each and every one of our seafarers: I know exactly how you feel!”

Was macht Silke Muschitz heute?

Sie muss einiges richtig gemacht haben in den vergangenen zwei Jahren, denn am 01.04.2022 wurde Silke Muschitz ein weiteres Mal befördert. Als „Head of Fleet Management“ ist sie jetzt Chefin der gesamten deutschen Flotte von Hapag-Lloyd und verantwortet sowohl die Betreuung der 1.300 Seeleute als auch das Gesamtmanagement aller Schiffe unter deutscher Flagge.

What’s Silke Muschitz doing today?

Muschitz must have done a lot right in the past two years, as she was promoted for a second time on 1 April 2022. As head of the entire own fleet, she is now responsible not only for looking after the 1,300 seafarers, but also for the overall management of all ships owned by Hapag-Lloyd.

TERMINAL BURCHARD
Hapag-Lloyd
YANG MING

„Wenn dein Schiff brennt, gehst du nicht ins Bett!“

Florian Böttger

“When your ship is on fire, you can’t just go to bed!”

Kapitän Florian Böttger fährt seit 17 Jahren für Hapag-Lloyd über die Meere – sechs davon als Kapitän. Hier erzählt er von seinen Anfängen auf schwedischen Autofähren, Ausflügen in Peru und Sydney und einem Brand an Bord der „Yantian Express", der ihm und seiner Besatzung alles abverlangte.

Captain Florian Böttger has been sailing for Hapag-Lloyd for 17 years – six of them as a master. Here, he talks about starting out on Swedish car ferries, excursions in Peru and Sydney, and a fire on board the "Yantian Express" that stretched him and his crew to the limit.

Brücke mit Ausblick: Kapitän Böttger auf der „Cartagena Express" am Hamburger Burchardkai

A bridge with a view: Böttger on the "Cartagena Express" at Hamburg's Container Terminal Burchardkai

<<

Crewwechsel am Hamburger Burchardkai. Kapitän Florian Böttger übergibt die „Cartagena Express" nach neun Wochen Südamerika-Loop seinem polnischen Kollegen Krzysztof Kaplon. „Leider hatten wir pandemiebedingt keinen Landgang in Südamerika, das ist schon hart für die Besatzung!", erzählt der Kapitän. „Aber mit gemeinsamen Barbecues, Sportturnieren und Filmabenden haben wir die freie Zeit ganz gut rumgekriegt." Jetzt freut er sich auf seine Familie, denn gleich geht es nach Bremen zu den Söhnen Ben und Nick. „Und natürlich freue ich mich auf meine Frau. Wir haben uns vor 22 Jahren auf meiner ersten Fahrt nach Südamerika kennengelernt, in Paita, Peru. Ich war damals noch Kadett und besuchte mit zwei Kollegen eine Diskothek. Adriana kam mit ein paar Freundinnen rein – es hat sofort gefunkt." Nicht schlecht, wenn man daheim in Deutschland eine Mutter mit Ballettschule hat, in der auch Salsa-Kurse gegeben werden:

Crew change at the Container Terminal Burchardkai in Hamburg. Captain Florian Böttger is handing over the "Cartagena Express" to his Polish colleague Krzysztof Kaplon after a nine-week round voyage to South America. "Unfortunately, we were unable to go ashore in South America due to the pandemic, which was pretty hard for the crew!" Böttger says. "However, we enjoyed our free time in other ways, with barbecues, sports tournaments and film evenings together."

Now he is looking forward to spending time with his family. Soon he will head to Bremen to see his sons, Ben and Nick. "And I'm looking forward to seeing my wife, of course. We met 22 years ago on my first voyage to South America in Paita, Peru. I was still a cadet at the time and had gone to a club with two colleagues. Adriana walked in with a

„Den Kurs hatte ich gerade hinter mir und forderte Adriana einfach zum Tanzen auf." Es muss ihr gefallen haben: Die Böttgers sind seit 16 Jahren glücklich verheiratet.

Auch die Seefahrt war Liebe auf den ersten Blick

Als kleiner Junge fuhr Florian Böttger regelmäßig mit seinen Eltern auf der Autofähre über Schweden nach Finnland, seine Mutter ist Finnin. „Die Überfahrten haben mich fasziniert", erzählt der heute 44-Jährige. Unzählige Ferien und Fährfahrten später bewarb sich der Abiturient an der Hochschule für Nautik in Bremen. Die nötige Ausbildung zum Nautischen Offiziersassistenten absolvierte er – wen wundert's – auf einer schwedischen Autofähre. „Nach sechs Monaten Travemünde-Trelleborg und zurück kannte ich allerdings jede Tonne auf der Ostsee. Ich wollte raus in die Welt, da kam nur die Containerschifffahrt infrage!"

Mit abgeschlossenem Studium und ersten Erfahrungen bei einer Bremer Reederei fragte Florian Böttger 2002 bei Hapag-Lloyd, ob sich eine Bewerbung lohne. „Der Herr am Telefon sagte aber nur: ‚Ich habe hier schon 200 Bewerber auf der Liste, soll ich Sie da noch drunter schreiben?' – ‚Nee, oben drüber!', antwortete ich etwas übermütig. Aber mir war klar, dass es der falsche Zeitpunkt war. Damals setzte Hapag-Lloyd noch auf das doppelte Patent. Das hatte ich nicht." So fuhr der gebürtige Hamburger bei den Reedereien Hansa Mare und Bertram Rickmers oft als einziger Deutscher mit Kroaten, Burmesen und Filipinos, bevor er 2005 einen zweiten Anlauf bei Hapag-Lloyd wagte. Diesmal funktionierte es.

Zwei Jahre fuhr er als Zweiter, dann folgte die Beförderung zum Ersten Offizier. „Wir waren gerade mit der ‚Maersk Dayton', heute die ‚Glasgow Express', unterwegs, als mein Chef gefragt wurde, ob er mir den

couple of friends, and we hit it off right away." It helps when your mother has a ballet school back in Germany that also offers salsa courses. "I had just finished the class and simply asked Adriana to dance." She must have been pleased, as the Böttgers have been happily married for 16 years.

> ***I wanted to go out into the world, so container shipping was my chance!***

It was also love at first sight with seafaring

As a small boy, Böttger travelled regularly with his parents by car ferry via Sweden to Finland, where his mother is from. "I was completely fascinated by the passages," recalls the 44-year-old. Countless holidays and ferry journeys later, he applied to study Nautical Sciences at the City University of Applied Sciences in Bremen right out of high school. The training required to become a nautical officer assistant took place on – no surprise – a Swedish car ferry. "However, after six months back and forth on the Travemünde-Trelleborg route, I knew every buoy on the Baltic Sea. I wanted to go out into the world, so container shipping was my chance!"

With a completed degree and initial work experience at a shipping company in Bremen, Böttger contacted Hapag-Lloyd in 2002 to ask whether an application would be worth his while. "The man on the phone simply said, 'I already have 200 applicants on the list. Shall I add you to the bottom?' – 'No, the top!' I replied, somewhat cockily. But it was clear to me that the timing was wrong. Hapag-Lloyd still required dual licences at the time. And I didn't have

Ersten Offizier zutraut. So wurde ich auf See befördert, hatte eine Woche Einarbeitungszeit und los ging's", erzählt Florian Böttger und erklärt: „Garbage- und Ballast-Management, Ladungskontrolle und die Stabilität des Schiffes, dazu Deck Maintenance – das war ein Riesenschritt." So sehr er in seinen Anfängen die Südamerika-Route liebte, lernte er jetzt die östliche Hemisphäre zu schätzen: „Von Singapur nach Freemantle, Melbourne, Sydney und zurück – alles großartige Städte und Häfen mit sehr entspannten Leuten!" Gern erinnert sich Böttger an diverse Ausflüge, so zum Beispiel den Besuch des Fernsehturms von Sydney: „Wenn du in 268 Meter Höhe auf dem Glasboden des Skywalks stehst und dir ganz Sydney zu Füßen liegt, das ist schon Wahnsinn", schwärmt er.

Den Brand auf der „Yantian Express" werde ich nie vergessen

Zwischen den Buchstaben lauern jede Menge Überraschungen

In seinen neun Jahren als Erster Offizier habe er die Welt, die Seefahrt, aber auch sich selbst besser kennengelernt. Ruhiger sei er geworden, er würde mehr nachdenken und als Kapitän auch die Meinungen anderer in seine Überlegungen mit einbeziehen. Florian Böttger: „Unser Job klingt ja erst mal recht einfach. Du musst ein Schiff sicher von Hafen A nach B nach C bringen. Aber zwischen den Buchstaben lauern jede Menge Überraschungen, auf die du jederzeit gefasst sein musst."

Eine dieser „Überraschungen" wird Florian Böttger nie vergessen: den Brand auf der „Yantian Express". „Es war der 2. Januar 2019, als mich der Zweite Offizier um Mitternacht aus dem Bett klingelte und auf die Brücke rief. Wir

them!" So the Hamburg native sailed for the shipping companies Hansa Mare and Bertram Rickmers, often as the only German alongside Croats, Burmese and Filipinos, before making a second attempt at Hapag-Lloyd in 2005. This time, he was successful.

Böttger sailed as second officer for two years before being promoted to chief officer. "We were travelling on board the 'Maersk Dayton', now the 'Glasgow Express', when my boss was asked whether he thought I was ready to be the chief officer. So I was promoted while at sea, had one week's training, and off I went," Böttger says, adding: "Garbage and ballast management, cargo control and ship stability, as well as deck maintenance – that was a huge step." And as much as he loved the South America route at the beginning, he now learned to appreciate the eastern hemisphere. "From Singapore to Fremantle, Melbourne, Sydney and back – they are all great cities and ports with very laid-back people!" Böttger fondly remembers various excursions, such as a visit to the TV tower in Sydney. "When you're standing on the glass floor of the Skywalk at a height of 268 metres and all of Sydney is beneath your feet, it's a crazy feeling," he says.

Plenty of surprises come along that you have to be ready to deal with

In his nine years as a chief officer, Böttger got to know the world, seafaring and even himself better. He became calmer and more thoughtful. And, as a captain, he includes the opinions of others in his considerations. "Our job sounds very easy at first. You have to bring a ship safely from port A to B to C," he says. "However, plenty of surprises come along

Die vielen Jahre auf See haben ihn ruhiger gemacht, sagt Florian Böttger. Anderen zuhören sei oft wichtiger, als alles allein zu entscheiden

Böttger says that his many years at sea have made him calmer, adding that listening to others is often more important than deciding everything on your own

>>

Kostbare Fracht: 11.519 Container passen auf die 333 Meter lange und 48 Meter breite „Cartagena Express". Aus Südamerika werden auf Ihr u. a. Kaffee, Kakao und Südfrüchte nach Europa gebracht

Precious cargo: 11,519 containers fit on the 333-metre-long and 48-metre-wide "Cartagena Express". Coffee, cocoa, tropical fruits and other goods are brought from South America to Europe

waren von Colombo nach Kanada, 800 Meilen südöstlich von Halifax unterwegs. Schon auf dem Weg zur Brücke sah ich das Leuchten auf dem Vorderschiff – ein Feuer war ausgebrochen. Und das in einer Bay, in der kein Gefahrgut deklariert war. Ich löste den Generalalarm aus, trommelte alle Seeleute an Deck." Die Mannschaft tat, was sie in so vielen Routine-Übungen geprobt hatte, nur dass es jetzt keine Übung, sondern ein Ernstfall war. „Die Männer hackten und bohrten Löcher in die Container, legten Feuerlöschschläuche aus, versuchten die

that you have to be ready to deal with at any time."

Böttger will never forget one of these "surprises": the fire on the "Yantian Express". "It was the 2nd of January 2019 at around midnight when the second officer called me out of bed to the bridge. We were on our way from Colombo to Canada, 800 miles south-east of Halifax. As I made my way to the bridge, I could already see the glow at the front of the ship – a fire had broken out. And it was in a bay where no dangerous goods had been declared. So I raised the general alarm and

^

brennenden Container zu fluten. Aber wir hatten das Wetter gegen uns, sieben bis acht Windstärken, die das Feuer immer wieder entfachten. Es schien aussichtslos, die Flammen sprangen einfach auf die nächstliegenden Container über.“ Drei Tage und Nächte bekämpfte die Besatzung ohne Pause das Feuer, schob sich immer wieder vor zu den Bränden. „Wir standen in engem Austausch mit dem Notfallteam an Land, ich hatte durchgehend telefonischen Kontakt zum Personalleiter Arnold Lipinski und seinem Team. ‚Herr Böttger, Sie müssen auch mal schlafen‘, mahnte er. Ich probierte es, stand aber zehn Minuten später wieder auf – wenn dein Schiff brennt, kannst du doch nicht ins Bett gehen!“ Kurze Zeit später gab es eine Explosion, das Feuer hatte sich auf die nächste Bay ausgebreitet und einen Gefahrgutcontainer entzündet. Auch der Frachtraum war schon betroffen. „Wir justierten dann die Strahlrohre so, dass sie eine Wasserwand erzeugten, damit sich das Feuer wenigstens nicht noch weiter nach Achtern ausbreitete.“

Inzwischen hatte Hapag-Lloyd einen Schlepper engagiert, der die Löscharbeiten von außen vorantrieb. Doch da sich das Wetter weiterhin verschlechterte, musste eine Entscheidung her. „Arnold Lipinski und sein Team schlugen vor, dass wir erst mal alle von Bord gehen, rauf auf den Schlepper und auf besseres Wetter warten.“

Er habe zunächst nur die Hälfte der Besatzung evakuiert, die Verbleibenden sollten die „Yantian Express“ am nächsten Tag zum Notabschleppen fertig machen. Dann gingen auch die restlichen Seemänner von Bord, als Letzter Florian Böttger: „Das Schiff zu verlassen, war der schlimmste Moment meiner Karriere. Aber ich hatte keine Wahl, zog den Überlebensanzug an und stieg auf die Lotsenleiter.“ Der Ausstieg gestaltete

called for all hands on deck.” The crew did what they had practised many times in routine drills; only now it was not a drill, but a serious situation. “The men hacked at and pierced holes in the containers, unrolled fire hoses and attempted to flood the burning containers. But we had the weather against us, and force-seven to -eight winds kept reigniting the fire. It seemed hopeless; the flames were simply jumping to the nearest containers”. For three days and nights, the crew battled the fire without interruption, pushing constantly towards the flames. “We liaised closely with the emergency team on land. I was in continuous phone contact with the human resources manager, Arnold Lipinski, and his team. ‘Mr Böttger, you also need to sleep,’ he warned. I tried to, but I was up again 10 minutes later. When your ship is on fire, you can’t just go to bed!”

A short time later, there was an explosion, as the fire had spread to the next bay and ignited a container carrying dangerous goods. The cargo hold was also already affected. “We adjusted the nozzles to create a wall of water so that the fire would at least not spread further towards the stern.” In the meantime, Hapag-Lloyd had commissioned a tug to help extinguish the fire from outside. However, as the weather continued to deteriorate, a decision had to be made. “Arnold Lipinski and his team suggested that we all disembark, get onto the tug, and wait for better weather.”

Böttger first evacuated just half the crew, while the remaining members prepared the “Yantian Express” for an emergency towing operation the next day. Then the rest of the seafarers disembarked, with Böttger being the last off the vessel. “Leaving the ship was the worst moment of my career. However, I had no choice, so I put on my survival suit and climbed onto the pilot ladder.” Disembarking proved to be more difficult than expected. “The

sich schwerer als gedacht: „Bei vier Meter hohen Wellen warf man mir vom Rettungsboot den Tampen zu, aber ich griff ins Leere, knallte rücklings mit der Leiter zurück an die Bordwand. Die 72 Stunden ohne Schlaf machten sich bemerkbar, ich konnte mich gerade noch fangen." Beim zweiten Mal funktionierte es, Böttger erwischte den Tampen und sprang in den Atlantik. „Das Rettungsboot zog mich volle Kraft voraus weg vom Schiff. Erst an Bord des Schleppers sah ich dann das ganze Ausmaß des Brandes: die brennenden Container und eine Rauchwolke, die kilometerweit in den Himmel stieg." Nach einer Lagebesprechung inklusive großem Lob für seine erschöpfte Besatzung fiel Florian Böttger in einen zehnstündigen traumlosen Schlaf.

Das Schiff zu verlassen, war der schlimmste Moment meiner Karriere

Endlich wieder an Bord, Happy End mit Uhr

Zwei Tage später klarte das Wetter auf und der nächste Schlepper erreichte die „Yantian Express", an Bord ein Salvage Master, der auf Brände an Bord spezialisiert ist. „Mit ihm, dem Chief Engineer, dem Ersten Offizier und dem Zweiten Ingenieur und unserem Auszubildenden bin ich dann wieder an Bord gegangen. Endlich konnten wir wieder arbeiten." Ein dritter Schlepper brachte eine komplette Salvage Crew aus Rotterdam. „Die haben in voller Montur Löcher in die Containerwände geschlagen, sind in die Container reingegangen, von einem zum nächsten." Die Besatzung der „Yantian Express" wechselte auf ein Schwesterschiff und konnte in Halifax von Bord gehen. Für Kapitän Böttger und seine Mitstreiter war noch lange

waves were four metres high and the line was thrown to me from the rescue boat, but I grabbed at the air and crashed backwards with the ladder against the side of the ship. The 72 hours without sleep were showing their effect; I was able to just catch myself."

Böttger was successful at the second try; he caught the line and jumped into the Atlantic. "The rescue boat pulled me away from the ship at full speed. It was only when I was on board the tug that I saw the full extent of the fire: the burning containers and a plume of smoke that stretched for kilometres up into the sky." After a debriefing that included high praise for his exhausted crew, Böttger fell into a deep and dreamless 10 hours of sleep.

Finally back on board

Two days later, the weather cleared. The next tug reached the "Yantian Express" with a salvage master on board who specialised in vessel fires. "I went aboard again with him, the chief engineer, the first officer, the second engineer and our apprentice. We were finally able to get back to work."

A third tug brought an entire salvage crew from Rotterdam. "Dressed in full protective gear, they punched holes in the container walls and went into the containers, one after the other." The crew of the "Yantian Express" moved to a sister ship and was able to disembark in Halifax. For Captain Böttger and his fellow combatants, the end was still a long way off. "The five of us remained on board and were able to steer our ship under its own power to Freeport, in the Bahamas. Small fires continued to flare up, and we only managed to extinguish them shortly before our arrival. On the 2nd of February, we disembarked."

The Executive Board was greatly

Aufhören nach dem Brand auf der „Yantian Express"? Für den leidenschaftlichen Seefahrer keine Option!

Quitting after the fire on the "Yantian Express"? Not an option for this passionate seafarer!

>>

nicht Schluss: „Wir fünf blieben an Bord, konnten unser Schiff mit eigener Kraft nach Freeport auf die Bahamas steuern, immer noch loderten kleine Brandherde, die erst kurz vor der Ankunft gelöscht werden konnten. Am 2. Februar sind wir von Bord gegangen."

Kapitän Böttgers Mut und sein besonnenes Handeln, die gute Zusammenarbeit mit der Crew und dem Notfallteam rund um Arnold Lipinski hat den Vorstand schwer beeindruckt. Alle Beteiligten wurden später an den Ballindamm eingeladen und gebührend geehrt. Stolz zeigt Kapitän Böttger die Uhr an seinem Handgelenk: „Die hat Anthony J. Firmin, damals noch im Vorstand, für uns ausgesucht. Eine Uhr, die speziell für Feuerwehrleute entwickelt wurde." Hat er nach dem Vorfall auf der „Yantian Express" jemals ans Aufhören gedacht? „Nicht eine Sekunde!", schüttelt Florian Böttger den Kopf. „Mich hat diese Erfahrung eher bestärkt. Was soll mich jetzt noch umhauen?", resümiert er und denkt an die Worte, die ihm Managing Director Richard von Berlepsch bei der Beförderung zum Kapitän mitgegeben hat: „Ihnen wird irgendwann etwas passieren, Herr Böttger. Am Anfang, in der Mitte oder am Ende ihrer Karriere. Egal wann, wir müssen auf Sie zählen können. Wenn wir die Kommunikation zu Ihnen verlieren, verlieren wir auch das Schiff." Die „Yantian Express" fährt wieder – und das hat sie maßgeblich Kapitän Florian Böttger zu verdanken.

impressed by Captain Böttger's courage, level-headedness, and strong teamwork with the crew and Arnold Lipinski's emergency team. All those involved were later invited to the Ballindamm in Hamburg and properly honoured.

Leaving the ship was the worst moment of my career

Böttger proudly displays the watch on his wrist. "Anthony J. Firmin, who was on the Executive Board at the time, picked these out for us. They're watches that were specially designed for firefighters." Did he ever think of giving up after the incident on the "Yantian Express"? "Not for a second!" Böttger says, shaking his head. "If anything, the experience made me stronger. What could possibly blow me away now?" he concludes, thinking of what Managing Director Richard von Berlepsch said to him when promoting him to captain: "At some point, something is going to happen to you, Mr Böttger – at the beginning, in the middle, or at the end of your career. Regardless of when it happens, we must be able to count on you. If we lose communication with you, we lose the ship – and that cannot happen under any circumstances."

The "Yantian Express" continues to sail, in no small part thanks to Captain Florian Böttger.

Was macht Florian Böttger heute?

In Finnland, der Heimat seiner Mutter, verbrachte Florian Böttger im Sommer drei Wochen mit seiner Familie in der Nähe von Tampere. „Wir waren oft Angeln mit den Jungs, haben uns eine beeindruckende Banksy-Ausstellung in den Serlachius Museen in Mänttä angeschaut, eine wunderbare Zeit!", erzählt Kapitän Böttger am Telefon. Seit September fährt er auf der „Cartagena Express" Richtung Südamerika und freut sich, dass die Mannschaft jetzt auch mal wieder Landgänge unternehmen kann.

What's Florian Böttger doing today?

In the summer, Böttger spent three weeks with his family near Tampere in Finland, where his mother is from. "We went fishing a lot with the boys and saw an impressive Banksy exhibition at the Serlachius Museums in Mänttä – a fantastic time!" Böttger says on the phone. Since September, he has been sailing on the "Cartagena Express" heading for South America and is happy that the crew can now also go on shore leaves again.

Auch Kapitäne werden seekrank

Björn Kropp

Even captains can get seasick

Seit 2012 steuert Björn Kropp Hapag-Lloyds Schiffe als Kapitän über die Meere. Mit seinen 33 Jahren gehörte er damals zu den Jüngsten Kapitänen der Reederei. Wie es dazu kam, warum die Seefahrt auch unverhoffte Familienzusammenkünfte ermöglicht und was der gebürtige Koblenzer mit der Romanfigur Horatio Hornblower gemeinsam hat, erzählt er hier.

Captain Björn Kropp has sailed on Hapag-Lloyd ships since 2012. When he was 33 years old, he was one of the shipping company's youngest captains. Here, he shares how that came about, why seafaring also makes unexpected family reunions possible, and what the native of Koblenz has in common with the novel character Horatio Hornblower.

Durchblick: Björn Kropp am Binnenhafen des beschaulichen Oldenburg in Niedersachsen

All things in sight: Kropp at the inland port of placid Oldenburg in Lower Saxony

<<

Die jüngste Fahrt mit der „Callao Express"? „Anstrengend!", erzählt Björn Kropp ebenso knapp wie freimütig. „Die Reise an sich war okay, das Wetter gut, aber vor der Küste Perus wurde ich mitten in der Nacht geweckt. Ein Matrose hatte Herzprobleme, Schmerzen in der Brust, die in den rechten Arm ausstrahlten", berichtet der 41-Jährige. „Wir setzen sofort alle Hebel in Bewegung, riefen auch das zuständige Krankenhaus in Cuxhaven an, das uns bei der Diagnose und Behandlung unterstützte. Da keine Besserung eintrat, empfahlen sie die zugige Evakuierung des Erkrankten." Die Kontaktaufnahme mit den peruanischen Behörden gestaltete sich allerdings schwierig – offenbar hatte sich die Nummer der 24-Stunden-Hotline geändert. „Erst mithilfe der Seenotleitung in Bremen, später dann der von Madrid, konnten wir einen Kontakt herstellen. Am nächsten Vormittag unterstützten uns dann unsere Hapag-Lloyd-Kollegen tatkräftig bei der

Exhausting!" is the honest and concise answer that Björn Kropp gives when asked how his last voyage on the "Callao Express" was. "The voyage itself was fine, and the weather was good. But I was woken up in the middle of the night off the coast of Peru. An ordinary seaman had heart problems as well as chest pains that were radiating to his right arm," the 41-year-old reports. "We immediately put everything in motion in addition to telephoning a hospital in Cuxhaven, which helped us with the diagnosis and treatment recommendations. But after there were no improvements, they advised us to quickly evacuate the ailing seafarer."

However, getting in touch with the Peruvian authorities turned out to be difficult, as the number of the 24-hour hotline had apparently changed. "We were only able to establish contact with the help of

Organisation und Kommunikation vor Ort – die machen einen super Job!“ Am Ende bekam Kapitän Kropp trotz vorheriger Ankündigung der peruanischen Behörden keinen Hubschrauber, sondern musste vor Chimbote, einem Industriehafen, ankern, um den Mann abholen zu lassen: Wie sich ein solcher Vorfall auf die Zusammenarbeit an Bord auswirkt? „Eigentlich sollen die Leute zwischendurch auch mal schlafen, denn die vielen Häfen an der Westküste sind arbeitsintensiv. Aber in dieser Situation sprang einer für den anderen ein: der Dritte Offizier übernahm die Wache von 0 bis 4 Uhr vom Zweiten Offizier, der sich im Bordhospital um den armen Kerl kümmerte, der Erste Offizier stand mit dem Krankenhaus in Cuxhaven in Verbindung, und ich kümmerte mich um die Kommunikation mit den zentralen Stellen an Land, der Seenotrettung, Hapag-Lloyd und der Agentur. Vor Chimbote mussten wir dann noch diskutieren, wie weit wir in den Hafen hineinfahren. Mit 14 Meter Tiefgang weigerte ich mich aus guten Grund“, erzählt der Kapitän. Am Ende sei alles glatt gelaufen: „Der Matrose kam rechtzeitig ins Krankenhaus, wurde behandelt und konnte von dort nach Hause auf die Philippinen fliegen.“

Wir besuchen den Kapitän in seiner Wahlheimat Oldenburg in Niedersachsen. Im Esszimmer hängen gerahmte Jugendstilplakate des Norddeutschen Lloyd und der Hamburg-Amerika-Linie in trauter Einheit, über der Anrichte gleitet die „London Express“ durchs Bild, ein Geschenk seiner Eltern zum ersten Einsatz als Kapitän. Und auf der Fensterbank thront ein weiteres Containerschiff. Das hat Björn Kropps Sohn in seiner Grundschulzeit aus Holz gebaut.

_____ Mit dem Fernglas auf Wangerooge, seekrank auf der „Wilhelmshaven“

Bereits als Kind saß er mit dem Fernglas

the Maritime Rescue Coordination Centre in Bremen and then the one of Madrid,” he continues. “The next morning, our local Hapag-Lloyd colleagues actively assisted with organisational and communication efforts. They really do a super job!”

Stage 1: You become seasick. Stage 2: You think you’re going to die. Stage 3: You don’t!

In the end, Captain Kropp did not get the helicopter that the Peruvian authorities said he would. Instead, the ship had to anchor off Chimbote, an industrial port, to have the seafarer picked up. When asked how incidents like this impact how everyone works together on board, he says: “People are actually supposed to get some sleep whenever they can because the many ports on the west coast are very labour-intensive. But, in this case, everyone helped each other out: The third officer took over the midnight-to-4-am watch for the second officer, who looked after the poor guy in the ship bay. The chief mate was in contact with the hospital in Cuxhaven. And I handled communications with the central offices ashore, the sea rescue service, Hapag-Lloyd and the agency. While anchored off Chimbote, we then had to discuss how far into the port we would sail. And given our 14-metre draught, I had good reasons for refusing to do so.” In the end, everything went smoothly, he adds, saying: “The ordinary seaman got to the hospital in time, received treatment for his condition, and was able to fly home to the Philippines from there.”

Our visit with the captain took place in his adopted home of Oldenburg, a city in north-western Germany west of Bremen. Hanging in the dining room is a harmoniously arranged set of Art

in den Händen am Strand von Wangerooge und beobachtete die Schiffe, die auf der Nordsee Richtung Weser fuhren: „,Ich will Kapitän werden!', soll ich gesagt haben. Das erzählen meine Eltern heute noch gern", grinst Kropp. Zwei Jahre später bekam der frühe Berufswunsch einen kleinen Dämpfer: „Auf der ,Wilhelmshaven', einem Seebäderschiff, mit dem wir einen Ausflug nach Helgoland unternahmen, wurde ich richtig seekrank", berichtet der gebürtige Koblenzer und erklärt augenzwinkernd die drei Stufen wahrer Seekrankheit: „Stufe 1: Du wirst seekrank, Stufe 2: Du denkst, du stirbst, Stufe 3: Du stirbst nicht!" Abgehalten hat ihn die Seekrankheit von seinem Beruf nicht. „Auf Containerschiffen ist mir das noch nie passiert."

Stufe 1: Du wirst seekrank, Stufe 2: Du denkst, du stirbst, Stufe 3: Du stirbst nicht!

Sein Geburtsort Koblenz ist für die Flüsse Rhein und Mosel, die hier ineinander münden, bekannt, aber zur Hochseeschifffahrt hat keiner aus der Familie einen Draht. „Aber ich war schon früh im Segelclub, bin mit dem Optimisten auf dem Stausee unterwegs gewesen", erzählt der Kapitän. Von da war es nicht weit zur ersten Segelfreizeit auf der Ostsee mit der historischen Gaffel-Ketsch „Seute Deern". Hier lernte Björn Kropp auch ein paar Seeleute kennen, die ehrenamtlich den Laden in Schwung hielten und denen fiel schnell auf, mit wie viel Leidenschaft sich der 16-Jährige ins Zeug legte. „Bewirb dich doch mal auf ein Ferienpraktikum beim ,Verband Deutscher Reeder', dann kannst du mit einem richtigen Schiff fahren", riet ihm einer der alten Seemänner. So landete Björn Kropp auf der „Nürnberg Express". „Sechs Wochen im Golf von Mexiko, lange

Nouveau posters of North German Lloyd and the Hamburg America Line. Above the sideboard is a picture of the "London Express" gliding across the ocean, which his parents gave him as a present after his first command as a captain. And perched on the windowsill is another container ship, which Kropp's son made out of wood in grade school.

With binoculars on the seashore, seasick on the "Wilhelmshaven"

As a young boy, Kropp was already sitting on the beach of the North Sea island of Wangerooge holding binoculars and watching the ships sail towards the Weser river. "Legend has it that I said: 'I want to be a captain!' My parents still like to tell that story today," he says with a grin. Two years later, a bit of a damper was put on his early career aspirations. "We were taking an excursion to Helgoland on board the 'Wilhelmshaven', a ship that stops at seaside resorts. But I got really seasick," recalls the native of the western German city of Koblenz before listing off the three stages of real seasickness with a wink: "Stage 1: You become seasick. Stage 2: You think you're going to die. Stage 3: You don't die!" But a bit of seasickness didn't keep him from pursuing his dream job. "In fact, it has never happened to me on a container ship," he notes.

Koblenz, the town he was born in, is where the Rhine and the Moselle rivers meet. But no one from his family has ever had any connection with ocean-going shipping. "I was in the sailing club from an early age, however, and I would go out on the reservoir with an Optimist dinghy," Kropp says. And it wasn't long before he had his first sailing holiday on the Baltic Sea on board the 'Seute Deern', a vintage gaff-rigged

Das Innere eines Containerschiffes gleicht einem Labyrinth. Auch wenn sich die Seeleute bestens auskennen, ist für den Fall der Fälle alles ausgeschildert

The inside of a container ship is like a labyrinth. Even if the seamen know their way around, everything is signposted to be on the safe side

>>

EXIT TO
GANGWAY

Björn Kropp verbrachte seine erste Zeit als Azubi auf einer Werft in Hongkong: „Da lernst du ein Schiff in- und auswendig kennen"

Kropp spent his early days as an apprentice at a shipyard in Hong Kong: "That's when you get to know a ship inside and out."

Hafenzeiten, großartige Ausflüge. Beim Festmachen helfen, Brücke und Maschine kennenlernen und dazu sogar ein bisschen Theorieunterricht – spätestens da war mir klar: Das ist mein Weg!" Und der führte ihn noch vor dem Abitur direkt zum dreistündigen Bewerbungsgespräch an den Ballindamm. Ein paar Wochen später kam das Go, der Schüler Kropp musste nur noch sein Abitur absolvieren.

Erst in die Werft, dann rund um den Globus

„Dass meine erste Fahrt als Azubi mit der

ketch. It was here that Kropp met a couple of seafarers who volunteered to keep the old ship in decent shape – and who quickly noticed how much passion the 16-year-old put into his work. One of the old sailors advised him: "Why don't you go and apply for a holiday internship with the German Shipowners' Association? Then you can sail on a real ship!"

And that's how Kropp ended up on board the "Nürnberg Express". "Six weeks in the Gulf of Mexico, long stays in ports, and great excursions," he recalls. "Helping with berthing, becoming familiar with the

‚Stuttgart Express' gleich nach Hongkong in die Werft ging, war für mich ein Glücksfall. In einem Trockendock lernst du ein Schiff buchstäblich in- und auswendig kennen – wann sonst kann man sich einen Schiffsrumpf schon mal gefahrlos von unten angucken? Auch Hongkong erkundeten wir ausgiebig. Das Gewusel in den Straßen, das unglaubliche U-Bahn-Netz, die fremden Gerüche. Ein Freund aus Koblenz lebte zudem dort, so hatte ich sogar meinen persönlichen Tour Guide. Eine Fahrt mit der Star Ferry von Kowloon nach Hongkong Island kann ich nur jedem empfehlen – die alten Fährboote haben es sogar in den einen oder anderen James-Bond-Film geschafft."

Nicht so actionreich wie im Kino, aber ebenso interessant verliefen Ausbildung und Studium des Seemanns. „Erst die Ost-Asien-Dienste, dann Amerika und das erste Mal durch den Panama Kanal mit den alten Treidelloks. Und auch die Ausflüge, beispielsweise in Los Angeles zu den Universal Studios, waren ein Erlebnis. Später hatte ich das Glück, als Erster Offizier die Route nach Australien und Neuseeland zu fahren – das war wirklich eine großartige Zeit!" Neuseeland findet der Kapitän auch historisch hochinteressant: „Die dramatische Terra-Nova-Expedition von R. F. Scott zum Südpol 1910 startete hier, bevor allesamt im Eis erfroren sind – unglaublich, was Menschen früher auf sich genommen haben! Wo du auch hinfährst, stolperst du über historische Namen und Ereignisse. Auch auf die Ursprünge unserer heutigen Globalisierung: Von Port Chalmers auf der Südinsel legte 1881 die ‚Dunedin' als eines der ersten Kühlschiffe weltweit Richtung London ab. Wenn ich überlege, wie viele Kühlcontainer heute unterwegs sind – das ist schon eine unglaubliche Entwicklung."

Die Route nach Neuseeland sorgte für eine Familienzusammenführung der

bridge and the engine room, and even a bit of theoretical training. By then at the latest, it was clear to me: This is the path for me!" And that led him directly to a three-hour apprenticeship interview at Hapag-Lloyd's headquarters on the Ballindamm even before he had finished high school. He got the green light just a few weeks later. And then the only thing he had left to do was pass his A-levels.

My first voyage went straight to the shipyard in Hong Kong – a stroke of luck!

First into the shipyard, then around the globe

"For me, the fact that my first voyage as an apprentice went straight to the shipyard in Hong Kong with the 'Stuttgart Express' was a stroke of luck," Kropp says. "In a dry dock, you literally get to know a ship inside out. I mean, when else do you get a chance to safely examine a ship's hull from below? And we also spent a lot of time exploring Hong Kong and experiencing the hustle and bustle in the streets, the incredible underground network and the unfamiliar smells. Plus, a friend of mine from Koblenz was living there, so I even had my own personal tour guide.
I can only recommend to everyone a trip on the Star Ferry from Kowloon to Hong Kong Island. The old ferry boats have even made it into a couple James Bond films."

Though perhaps not as action-packed as one sees in the movies, his practical training and theoretical coursework to become a seafarer were still very interesting. "First the East Asia services, then America, and then through the Panama Canal with the old electric towing locomotives," he says. "And then the onshore

besonderen Art: „Meine Schwester und ich haben beide in Elsfleth studiert, sie mit dem Schwerpunkt Logistik. Nach dem Studium ist sie nach Auckland ausgewandert. Ich war der Erste aus der Familie, der sie dann mal schnell auf einen Kaffee besuchte!", lacht Björn Kropp.

Plötzlich bist du mit deinen Zweifeln allein, musst dich aber entscheiden

Mit Hurrikan „Sandy" zum ersten Einsatz als Kapitän

Nach gut sechs Jahren als Erster Offizier war es dann so weit. Björn Kropp: „Ich sollte die ‚London Express' in New York übernehmen und eine Übergabefahrt über Halifax bis nach Hamburg machen. Aber Hurrikan ‚Sandy' hatte die halbe Ostküste verwüstet und unzählige Verspätungen verursacht. So verkürzte sich die Übergabe von sieben Tagen auf 40 Stunden von New York nach Halifax, wo der andere Kapitän, ebenfalls ein Neuling, ausstieg. Ab da war ich auf mich gestellt." Unzählige Male hatte Björn Kropp bis dahin schon An- und Ablegemanöver gefahren. „Aber wenn du da plötzlich allein stehst, ist es noch mal was völlig anderes. Du bist auch mit deinen Zweifeln allein und musst doch die richtige Entscheidung treffen. Als in Antwerpen plötzlich weit und breit kein Lotse zu sehen war, dachte ich sofort, ich sei schuld – aber es war einfach keiner gekommen." Heut blickt Björn Kropp mit einem Lächeln auf seine Anfangszeit als Kapitän zurück. „Es ist wie mit dem Panama Kanal: Die erste Durchfahrt ist aufregend, aber wenn du sechsmal im Jahr durchfährst, gewöhnst du dich daran. Heute schau ich viel mehr auf die Mannschaft, versuche bei den Leuten zu sein und zuzuhören. Aus meiner Zeit als

excursions were also an adventure, such as the one to Universal Studies in Los Angeles. Later, I was lucky enough to sail on the Australia and New Zealand route as a chief mate. It was a really fantastic time!"

The captain also finds the history of New Zealand extremely fascinating. "R.F. Scott's dramatic Terra Nova Expedition to the South Pole started here in 1910, though they would eventually all freeze to death in the ice. It's unbelievable the kind of challenges that people used to take on!" Kropp says. "Wherever you go, you stumble across names and events of historical importance – not to mention the origins of today's globalisation. In 1881, the 'Dunedin' set sail for London from Port Chalmers on the South Island as one of the world's first refrigerated ships. When I think about how many reefers are out there today, that's quite an incredible development!" The route to New Zealand facilitated a special kind of family reunion. "My sister and I both studied in Elsfleth, where she majored in Logistics," he continues, referring to a town between Bremen and Bremerhaven that is home to a well-known school of navigation. "She moved to Auckland after graduating," he continues, adding with a laugh that he was "the first one in the family to visit her for a quick coffee".

Becoming a captain during a devastating hurricane

After a bit more than six years as a chief officer, the big day had finally arrived. "I was supposed to take command of the 'London Express' in New York and have a handover voyage to Hamburg via Halifax," Kropp recounts. "But Hurricane Sandy had devastated half the US East Coast and caused an enormous number of delays. This shortened the handover from seven days to 40 hours and only from New York to Halifax, where the other captain, who had also only been recently promoted,

Offizier weiß ich noch sehr genau, dass sich nicht jeder traut, eventuelle Missstände oder Konflikte offen anzusprechen. Ich glaube aber, dass das sehr wichtig für ein gutes Arbeitsklima ist."

Ausgleich findet der Kapitän auf dem Laufband und beim Lesen. Empfehlen kann er „Horatio Hornblower", eine elfbändige Romanreihe, in der er immer wieder gern liest. „In den Büchern von C. S. Forester geht's um einen jungen Fähnrich, der in der Zeit der Napoleonischen Kriege Anfang des 19. Jahrhunderts allerhand Abenteuer bestehen muss, bis er Admiral wird." Der Bestseller wurde 1951 mit Gregory Peck in der Hauptrolle und später auch fürs Fernsehen verfilmt. Zentrales Thema sind die vielen einsamen Entscheidungen, die ein Kapitän immer wieder zu fällen hat. „In den Geschichten steckt viel Wahres über das Leben auf See", findet Björn Kropp. Was der Kapitän im Interview nicht verrät, ist eine Eigenschaft, die er mit dem Romanhelden teilt: Auch Horatio Hornblower wird zu Beginn seiner Fahrten immer wieder seekrank. Auf einem Containerschiff wäre ihm das vermutlich nicht passiert.

disembarked. From that point on, I was on my own." By then, the new captain had already made countless berthing and casting-off manoeuvres. "But when you suddenly find yourself alone, it's something completely different," Kropp says. "You are alone with your doubts, but you still have to make the right decision."

Today, Kropp looks back fondly on his early days as a captain. "It was just like it was with the Panama Canal: The first passage is exhilarating. But once you start going through it six times a year, you get used to it," he says. "Today, I focus much more on the team aspects, and I try to spend time with and listen to others."

The captain unwinds by running on the treadmill and reading. He recommends the multi-volume series of Horatio Hornblower novels that he likes to reread every so often. "These books by C.S. Forester are about a young midshipman who has to go through all kinds of adventures before becoming an admiral during the Napoleonic Wars in the early 19th century," Kropp explains. A film adaptation of the best-selling series featuring Gregory Peck in the leading role was made in 1951, and later there was also a television adaptation. The central theme is the many lonely decisions that a captain has to make again and again. "There's a lot of truth in these stories about life at sea," Kropp notes. During the interview, the captain does not reveal a trait that he shares with the hero of this series of novels: Horatio Hornblower also repeatedly gets seasick during his early voyages – something that presumably wouldn't have happened to him on a container ship.

Was macht Björn Kropp heute?

Mit der „Callao Express" musste er kürzlich mehrere Tage in der Deutschen Bucht ankern, um einen Liegeplatz in Hamburg zu bekommen. „Die weltweiten Störungen des Warenverkehrs führen immer noch zu Verspätungen", schreibt er per Mail. „Um die Besatzung bei Laune zu halten, haben wir das hochsommerliche Wetter am Ankerplatz neun nautische Meilen südwestlich von Helgoland genutzt, um in der Nordsee schwimmen zu gehen. Das war ein sehr besonderes Erlebnis."

What's Björn Kropp doing today?

Kropp recently had to anchor for several days in the German Bight with the "Callao Express" before getting a berth in Hamburg. "Global disruptions to the movement of goods are still causing delays," he wrote via email. "To keep the crew's spirits up, we took advantage of the mid-summer weather at the anchorage nine nautical miles southwest of Helgoland to go swimming in the North Sea. It was a very special experience."

Wendezeiten aus der Ferne erlebt

Frank-Jürgen Schmidt

Far out at sea while history is being made at home

Er liest lieber John Irving und Thomas Mann statt Krimis, zieht Dorf und Gartenarbeit der Großstadt vor und bezeichnet sich selbst als Feministen: Kapitän Frank-Jürgen Schmidt fuhr 45 Jahren zur See, 27 davon für Hapag-Lloyd. Hier erzählt er von Lehrjahren und Wendezeiten und warum er zwei Mal für zehn Wochen mit der Aktentasche in Südkorea unterwegs war.

He prefers to read John Irving and Thomas Mann instead of crime novels, likes gardening in a village more than living in a big city, and describes himself as a feminist: Captain Frank-Jürgen Schmidt sailed for 45 years, 27 of them for Hapag-Lloyd. Here, he speaks about his years as an apprentice, about the period when the Berlin Wall fell and Germany reunited, and about finding himself in South Korea twice for 10 weeks each carrying a briefcase instead of commanding a ship.

Ost und West – Kapitän Frank-Jürgen Schmidt erlebte in 45 Jahren beide Seiten der deutschen Seefahrt

East and West – Captain Schmidt's 45 years in seafaring have been spent in both divided and reunified Germany

<<

Kindheit und Jugend habe ich in Ostberlin verlebt, da gab es einen Seesport-Marinestützpunkt, wo man segeln und rudern konnte. Dort entstand auch der Wunsch, zur See zu fahren. Es war damals die einzige Möglichkeit, die Welt zu sehen", erzählt Frank-Jürgen Schmidt. Der damals 17-jährige Ostberliner machte eine Ausbildung als Vollmatrose der Handelsschifffahrt, absolvierte sein Fachabitur und studierte schließlich Nautik in Warnemünde/Wustrow. Schmidt macht keinen Hehl daraus, dass er früh in die SED eingetreten war. „Ich war jung, hatte Ideale, dachte, ich könnte helfen, die Welt besser zu machen."

Die ersten Reisen mit dem Lehrschiff gingen nach Kuba, die frühen Jahre als Matrose verbrachte er auf Kümos entlang der europäischen Küsten. Seine erste große Fahrt auf dem Stückgutfrachter „Halle" führte den frisch beförderten Dritten Offizier in den Persischen Golf und nach Indien. Und auf dieser Fahrt

I spent my childhood and youth in East Berlin, where there was a naval base with an area where you could practice water sports, such as sailing and rowing. That's also where my desire to go to sea arose. Back then, it was the only way to see the world," recounts Frank-Jürgen Schmidt. The then-17-year-old started his apprenticeship to become an able seaman in merchant shipping, graduated from his vocational high school, and then went on to study Nautical Sciences at the maritime university in Warnemünde/Wustrow, on the Baltic Sea. Schmidt makes no secret of the fact that he joined early on the SED, the communist party that ruled the German Democratic Republic (GDR), also known as East Germany. "I was young, I had ideals, and I thought I could help make the world a better place," he says.

lauerten unzählige Herausforderungen: „Technische Ausfälle, Ladungsschäden, ein Streik der Hafenarbeiter in Kuwait und die bis heute ungeklärte Verminung des Seewegs im südlichen Roten Meer, das hatte ich so noch nicht erlebt", erzählt Kapitän Schmidt: „Zudem herrschte Anfang der 1980er-Jahre der Golfkrieg zwischen dem Irak und dem Iran und die Häfen waren im Ausnahmezustand. Dann gerieten wir noch in einen Monsun und hingen schließlich drei Wochen in Kalkutta fest." Kapitän Schmidt fand das alles eher spannend als beängstigend.

Mauerfall auf dem Indischen Ozean

In der DDR-Schifffahrt war manches anders, als später nach der Wende: „Es waren ausschließlich Deutsche an Bord und Landgang als Einzelperson war verboten", berichtet der 65-Jährige. Auch mit Alkohol wurde anders umgegangen. Der war streng limitiert, nur alle zehn Tage gab es eine Flasche Schnaps pro Mann, „Da wusste man schon im Voraus, wann mit der Mannschaft nichts anzufangen war", erzählt der Kapitän.

Die Wende 1989 erlebte Frank-Jürgen Schmidt mitten in der Nacht auf dem Indischen Ozean. „Am 4. Oktober fuhren wir von Rostock los, am 7. Oktober lagen wir in Bremen. Da wurde uns noch ein Blumenstrauß zum 40. Bestehen der DDR von unserem lokalen Agenten in die Hand gedrückt. Dann ging es Richtung Indien. Als ich am 9. November auf Wache kam, begrüßte mich der Zweite Offizier mit den Worten: ‚Die Mauer ist offen!'. Meine erste Reaktion weiß ich noch genau. Ich dachte: ‚Jetzt kann ich auch mal im Wannsee baden gehen und mit meinem Trabant um die Siegessäule fahren!' Genau das habe ich später getan."

Erst im März 1990 kamen Schiff und Crew nach Deutschland zurück.

His first voyages on a training vessel took him straight to Cuba, and he spent his early years as a seaman on vessels sailing along the coasts of Europe. His first really big voyage, which he took on the general cargo ship "Halle" as a freshly promoted third officer, took him to the Persian Gulf and then on to India. Countless challenges were awaiting him on this voyage. "Equipment breakdowns, damaged cargo, a dockworker strike in Kuwait, and the still-unexplained mining of the sea route in the southern Red Sea – I'd never experienced anything like that before," Captain Schmidt recalls. "On top of that, in the early 1980s, the Iran-Iraq War was still raging and the ports were under a state of emergency. Then we ran into a monsoon, which ultimately kept us in Calcutta for three weeks." But instead of finding all this frightening, Captain Schmidt found it exciting.

What I liked was that nobody stigmatised me for being an East German

On the Indian Ocean as the Berlin Wall falls

Of course, some things were different in GDR shipping than they were later after German reunification. "There were only Germans on board, and it was forbidden to go on shore alone," the 65-year-old recounts. Alcohol was also handled differently. It was strictly limited, and each man only received a bottle of schnapps every 10 days. "That meant you already knew beforehand when you wouldn't be able to get much done with the crew," the captain recounts.

When the Berlin Wall fell in 1989, Schmidt was at sea on the Indian Ocean in

„Meine Frau und mein Sohn besuchten mich dann in Bremen. Die Demonstrationen zu Hause in der DDR waren da bereits abgeklungen, jetzt sah ich nur überall Leute mit Einkaufstüten statt mit Plakaten und politischen Forderungen", erzählt Frank-Jürgen Schmidt und kann sich ein Grinsen nicht verkneifen. Schmidt gehört zu den wenigen, die dazu stehen, dass sie nicht ausschließlich von der neuen Freiheit begeistert waren. „So schnell wie manche Leute umgeschwenkt sind, das konnte doch gar nicht sein!"

Mit den ersten Entlassungswellen der DSR ahnte der damals 31-Jährige, dass er sich einen neuen Job suchen musste. Seine erste Anlaufstelle: Hapag-Lloyd. „Ich dachte, ich fang oben an, Abstriche kann ich immer noch machen." Auf seine Bewerbung erhielt er erst eine Absage, aber dann, wenige Monate später kam mit der Post die Aufforderung, seinen Arbeitsvertrag zu unterschreiben. „Ein richtiges Vorstellungsgespräch hat es nicht gegeben", lacht der sonst eher zurückhaltende Mann.

Mit doppeltem Patent an die Spitze

Mit Hapag-Lloyd begann für Frank-Jürgen Schmidt eine neue Zeit. „Adäquate Bezahlung und gute Rahmenbedingungen waren das eine. Aber am besten gefiel mir, dass mich niemand stigmatisierte als Ostdeutschen! Das Gegenteil war der Fall, damals hatte Hapag-Lloyd sogar Nachwuchssorgen." Als Zweiter Offizier stieg er ein, dann hängte er noch ein Studium für das technische Patent dran. „Die Idee war damals, dass man mit Doppelpatent sowohl auf der Brücke als auch in der Maschine Verantwortung übernimmt. Ich fand das spannend. Aber als ich dann nach dem Studium als Zweiter Ingenieur an Bord und auch noch alleiniger Elektriker vom Dienst war, merkte ich: Das ist alles gut zu wissen, aber nicht meins."

the middle of the night. "We sailed from Rostock on 4 October and berthed in Bremen on 7 October. There, our local agent gave us a bouquet of flowers to mark the 40th anniversary of the GDR. Then we set sail for India. When I came on watch on 9 November, the chief mate greeted me with the words: 'The Wall is open!' I can still clearly remember my initial reaction. I thought: 'Now I can go for a swim in the Wannsee and ride my Trabant around the Siegessäule!' [editor's note: The Wannsee is a lake in southwestern Berlin that was part of West Germany during the Cold War; a Trabant was the typical car in the GDR; and the Siegessäule is a tall Prussian victory monument in what was then West Berlin.] And that's exactly what I later did."

The ship and its crew did not get back to East Germany until March 1990. "My wife and son came to meet me in Bremen. The demonstrations at home in the GDR were already over, and now I only saw people everywhere with shopping bags instead of posters with political demands," Schmidt says with an insuppressible smile. Schmidt is one of the rare former inhabitants of the GDR who will openly admit that his enthusiasm about his newfound freedom was tinged with other emotions. "You just couldn't believe how quickly some people switched sides," he says.

When the DSR, the state-owned shipping company of the GDR, started making its first rounds of layoffs, the then-31-year-old suspected that it might be time to start looking for a new job. And the first place he went was Hapag-Lloyd. "I thought I'd start at the top, and that I could always lower my sights," he says. His application was initially rejected. But then, a few months later, he received a letter asking him to sign an

Warum Hapag-Lloyd? „Ich dachte, ich fange mal oben an", erzählt Kapitän Schmidt über seine Bewerbung

Why Hapag-Lloyd? "I thought I'd start at the top," Schmidt says about why he applied there first

>>

Welcher Hafen ihm besonders gefiel? „New Orleans! Die bunte Szene im French Quarter, die Jazzmusik – großartig", schwärmt Kapitän Schmidt

What has been his favourite port? "New Orleans! The colourful scene in the French Quarter, the jazz music – just terrific!" Schmidt says

Mit 41 wurde Schmidt als erster Ostdeutscher bei Hapag-Lloyd Kapitän. „Wenn du plötzlich der Chef an Bord bist, guckst du dir die See- und Wetterkarten natürlich noch mal genauer an, und mit deinen Zweifeln bist du erst mal allein. Aber ich empfand das als gute Herausforderung!" Das Führen der Crew bezeichnet er als unkompliziert. „Klar musste ich in seltenen Fällen durchgreifen. Einmal schickten wir einen Koch nach Hause, weil das Essen ungenießbar war, ein anderes Mal gab es eine Schlägerei an Bord. Ich beendete sie, indem ich den Angreifer

employment contract. "There hadn't even been a real interview," laughs the otherwise rather reserved man.

Taking two patents to the top

At Hapag-Lloyd, Schmidt began a new chapter of his life. "Adequate pay and good basic conditions were one thing," he continues. "But what I liked best was that nobody stigmatised me for being an East German! It fact, it was the opposite, as Hapag-Lloyd was even having trouble finding new employees at the time." After starting out as a second officer, he also

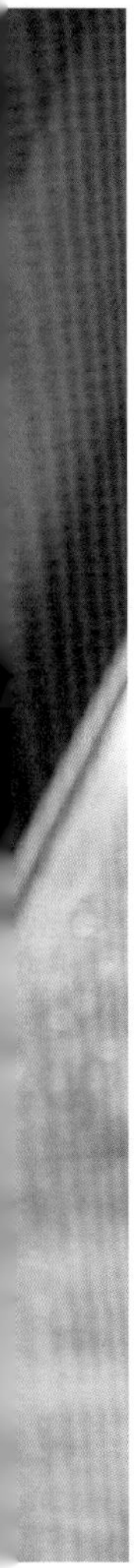

ins Bett schickte. Erst hinterher habe ich bemerkt, dass da ein Messer im Spiel war. Aber solche Situationen blieben die Ausnahme.“

Und welche Häfen gefielen ihm besonders? „New Orleans! Die bunt gemischte Szene im French Quarter, die Jazzmusik – großartig“, schwärmt Schmidt. „Aber auch Singapur ist und bleibt ein einmaliger Hafen. Wie die Leute es dort schaffen, so viele Nationalitäten unter einen Hut zu bringen, das ist schon beeindruckend.“

____ Mit der Aktentasche auf die Werft und wieder zurück

Besonders gern erinnert sich der Kapitän auch an den Neubau der „Tsingtao Express“ 2007 und der „Hamburg Express“, 2012 , die er jeweils zehn Wochen lang in Ulsan, Südkorea, begleiten durfte: „Zu sehen, wie von Anfang bis Ende ein Schiff entsteht, wie alle Teile zu einem werden, ist faszinierend. Die „Hamburg Express“ war damals das größte Containerschiff unter deutscher Flagge!“, erzählt Frank-Jürgen Schmidt stolz. Fast drei Monate dort an Land zu leben war für ihn besonders: „Ich ging morgens zur Arbeit, begutachtete mit dem fünfköpfigen Team, ob auch alles so gebaut wurde, wie es sein soll, und ging abends mit der Aktentasche unterm Arm nach Hause – so ein Leben kannte ich gar nicht.“

Kapitän Schmidt charakterisiert sich selbst als eher nordisch kühlen Typ, der lieber liest, als in großer Runde zu feiern. Literatur bleibt – neben der Gartenarbeit daheim bei Wittenberge – seine große Leidenschaft: „Isabel Allende, John Irving, aber auch die deutschen Klassiker wie Heinrich und Thomas Mann mag ich. Von Irving hat mich am meisten ‚Gottes Werk und Teufels Beitrag‘ fasziniert. Dass Irving Feminist ist, beeindruckt mich.“ Würde sich Kapitän Schmidt selbst als

began to study for an engineering license on top of his nautical one. “At the time, the idea was that, with both certificates, you could take charge not only on the bridge, but also in the engine room. I thought it was really exciting,” Schmidt recounts. “But then, after my studies, when I was second mate on board as well as the only electrician on duty, I realised that all of this was good to know – but it wasn’t my cup of tea.”

At the age of 41, Schmidt became the first former East German to become a captain at Hapag-Lloyd. “When you are suddenly the boss on board, you naturally take a closer look at the nautical and weather charts and with a completely different eye, and you are alone with your doubts,” he says. “But I thought it was a good challenge!” As Schmidt sees it, leading a crew isn’t all that complicated. “I obviously also had rare cases when I would have to take drastic measures,” he recalls. “For example, once we had to send a cook home because the food was inedible, and once there was a brawl on board. I broke it up by ordering the one who had started it to go to bed. It wasn’t until afterwards that I realised a knife had been involved. But those kind of situations were the exception.”

When asked about his favourite ports, Schmidt answers enthusiastically: “New Orleans! The colourful mixed scene in the French Quarter, the jazz music – just terrific! But Singapore has always been a unique port, too. It’s really impressive how the people there manage to reconcile so many nationalities.”

____ To the shipyard and back again with a briefcase

Other memories include the building of two new vessels – the “Tsingtao Express” in 2007 and the “Hamburg Express” in 2012 – which he was able to monitor in person for 10 weeks each time in Ulsan,

Feministen bezeichnen? „Ich bin schon sehr für die Gleichberechtigung, insofern habe ich damit kein Problem", sagt er. Kolleginnen an Bord hat er immer geschätzt: „Frauen reagieren besonnener und haben eine ausgleichende Wirkung", findet der Kapitän.

Mir gefiel, dass mich niemand als Ostdeutschen stigmatisierte

Seinen eigenen Ausgleich findet Frank-Jürgen Schmidt heute nicht mehr im Blau der Ozeane, sondern im Grün seines 2000 Quadratmeter großen Gartens, der dörflichen Idylle und bei seiner Familie. Seit dem 19. Oktober 2018 genießt er seinen Ruhestand und kümmert sich um seine zwei Enkel.

South Korea. "It's fascinating to see how a ship is built from start to finish," Schmidt says, noting that the "Hamburg Express" was the biggest container ship in the world under German flag at the time. Living on shore in South Korea for almost three months was something special for him. "I went to work in the morning, checked in with the five-man team to see if everything was being built as it should be, and went home in the evening with my briefcase under my arm," Schmidt recounts.

Captain Schmidt characterises himself as a rather reserved Nordic type who prefers to read rather than celebrate in large groups. Besides gardening at home near the northern German town of Wittenberge, his great passion is literature. "I like Isabel Allende and John Irving, but I also like the German classics, such as Heinrich and Thomas Mann," he says. "The Irving novel that fascinated me the most was 'The Cider House Rules.' I was impressed that Irving is both a man and a feminist." Would Captain Schmidt call himself a feminist? "I'm very much in favour of equality, so I don't have a problem with that," he says. In fact, he has always appreciated having women co-workers on board. "Women react in a more cool-headed way and have a balancing effect," he says.

Today, rather than on the blue seas, Schmidt finds his balance in his green 2,000-square-metre garden in an idyllic village with his family. Since retiring on 19 October 2018, he has been taking care of his two grandchildren.

Was macht Frank-Jürgen Schmidt heute? Seine beiden Enkel, mittlerweile vier und neun Jahre alt, halten Frank-Jürgen Schmidt ordentlich auf Trab, zum Beispiel bei der Schatzsuche, die er in seinem großen Garten organisiert. Außerdem sind die Schmidts in der Ukraine-Hilfe aktiv und engagieren sich in der Kommunalpolitik der Gemeinde Breese. Ihre Reisepläne mussten sie durch Corona verschieben, aber immerhin war schon ein zweiwöchiger Frankreichtrip drin. Und die nächste Reise ist bereits in Planung: Im Januar geht's endlich nach Tansania.

What's Frank-Jürgen Schmidt doing today? His two grandchildren, now four and nine years old, are keeping Schmidt on his toes, for example during treasure hunts that he organises especially for them in his large garden. In addition, the Schmidts are active in efforts to assist Ukrainians and local politics in Breese. The coronavirus pandemic forced the couple to postpone their travel plans, but at least a two-week trip to France is already on the agenda. And the next trip is already being planned, as they will finally be heading to Tanzania in January 2023.

Kapitän, Fotograf und stolzer Vater

Uwe Fiedler

Captain, photographer and proud father

Uwe Fiedler ist nicht nur Kapitän, sondern auch Hobbyfotograf mit eigener Website. Beim Durchklicken der Fotos ahnt man: Der Mann war auf der ganzen Welt unterwegs und hat ein Auge für ungewöhnliche Motive. Eine Begegnung an den Hamburger Landungsbrücken.

In addition to being a captain, Uwe Fiedler is also an amateur photographer with his own website. If you click through his photos, you might get the feeling that the man has been travelling all over the world and has a good eye for unusual scenes. An encounter at the Landungsbrücken jetty in Hamburg.

Ahoi! Uwe Fiedler ist bekannt für seine klaren Ansagen – und für die leckeren Waffeln, die er sonntags für die Besatzung backt

Ahoy! Fiedler is known for his clear instructions – and for the delicious waffles he makes for the crew on Sundays

<<

Wie viele seiner Kolleginnen und Kollegen wurde Fiedler früh mit dem Seefahrervirus infiziert: „Mein Vater war Kapitän und nahm mich schon als Vierjährigen mit an Bord. Ihm gehörte die ‚Göteborg', ein Küstenmotorschiff Baujahr 1948, mit dem er vorwiegend auf der Nord- und Ostsee unterwegs war." Der heute 66-Jährige erinnert sich gern an die unzähligen Sommerferien auf See. „Bei uns zu Hause hängt noch ein Foto an der Wand, das mich als kleinen Jungen eingemummelt in Decken zwischen meinen großen Schwestern auf dem Lukendeckel zeigt."

Gleich nach dem Abitur verpflichtete sich der 18-Jährige bei der Bundesmarine, lernte dort in acht Jahren als Navigator die Seefahrt von der strengeren Seite kennen: „Da herrschte eine strikte Hierarchie und ein mitunter rauer Ton." Mit dieser Erfahrung und dem anschließenden Studium fürs Nautische Patent konnte es mit der Handelsmarine auf

Like many of his colleagues, Uwe Fiedler got the seafaring bug early on. "My father was a captain, and he took me on board when I was only four. He owned the 'Göteborg', a coaster built in 1948, and he mainly sailed on the North and Baltic seas." The 66-year-old fondly recalls the countless summer holidays spent at sea. "At our house, there's still a photo on the wall showing me as a young boy wrapped in blankets sitting between my big sisters on the hatch cover."

Right after graduating from high school, the then-18-year-old enlisted in the German Navy, where he spent eight years as a navigator learning seafaring in a much more disciplined environment. "There was a strict hierarchy, and sometimes things were said in a harsh tone." With this experience and his subsequent studies to obtain his nautical license,

in die ganze Welt gehen. „Ich habe den kompletten Wandel der Schifffahrt in den vergangenen Jahrzehnten mitgemacht, kenne noch die Zeit, als man mit Sextant und Sichtfunkpeiler navigierte. Heute bekommt man seine Position in Sekundenschnelle per GPS gemeldet." Uwe Fiedler will nichts hören von „Früher war alles besser": „Es war einfach anders, das kann man gar nicht vergleichen. Klar ist heute mehr Papierkram und die riesigen Containerschiffe fordern dich. Andererseits darf man die harten Bedingungen damals auch nicht vergessen. Da gab es weder Einzelkabinen noch Klimaanlage. Auch die körperliche Arbeit war anspruchsvoller."

Kostbare Fracht, Mülltrennung und Bierflaschen für 150 Dollar

Die frühen Jahre haben den Zweimetermann mit den stahlgrauen Augen geprägt. „Ich würde mich als eher strengen Kapitän bezeichnen", erzählt er. „Als Kopf der Mannschaft trägst du eine unglaubliche Verantwortung. Der Wert eines beladenen Schiffs kann bis zu einer Milliarde betragen, wenn da die Crew nicht funktioniert, hast du ein echtes Problem." Dennoch sei es wichtig, dass man sich immer wieder reflektiert. „Du bist ja allein als Chef. Da muss man aufpassen, dass man sich nicht überschätzt."

Ein guter Zusammenhalt sei unerlässlich, findet Fiedler. Und dabei hilft ihm auch seine langjährige Erfahrung: „Kapitän ist einer der wenigen Berufe, wo du im Alter immer besser wirst. Viele Entscheidungen treffe ich aus dem Bauch heraus, da muss ich gar nicht mehr nachdenken." Seine Erfahrung hat ihn auch gelehrt, dass Tempo nicht alles ist, vor allem nicht bei schlechtem Wetter: „Ich komme lieber zu spät und heil an als pünktlich und zertrümmert", fasst er seine Einstellung zusammen. Dennoch geriet auch Fiedler mit seinen Schiffen in den

Fiedler was able to join the merchant marine and see the entire world. "I've witnessed first-hand how shipping has completely transformed in recent decades, and I remember the time when people navigated using a sextant and visual radio direction finder. Today, a GPS device tells you your position in a matter of seconds."

Ship master is one of the few professions where you get better with age

Fiedler does not want to hear about how much better things were in the old days. "It was just different – you can't compare it," he says. "Of course, there's more paperwork now, and the giant container ships are a challenge. On the other hand, we shouldn't forget how hard conditions were back then. There were no single cabins and no air conditioning, and the physical work was more demanding, too."

Precious cargo, waste separation and beer bottles for $150

Those early years had a lasting influence on this 2-metre-tall man with steel-grey eyes. "I'd describe myself as a rather strict captain," he says. "As the head of the crew, you bear an incredible amount of responsibility. A loaded ship can be worth up to a billion dollars, and if the crew isn't functioning well, you have a real problem on your hands." Nevertheless, he adds, it's important to always think about yourself, too. "After all, you're alone as the boss. You have to be careful not to overestimate yourself."

Fiedler believes a solid team spirit is crucial – and his many years of experience also help. "Ship master is one of the few professions where you get better with age," he says. "I make many decisions

einen oder anderen Sturm – zum Beispiel auf der Tasmanischen See, der Meerenge zwischen Australien und Tasmanien, wo Pazifischer und Indischer Ozean aufeinandertreffen und extrem hohe Wellen gehen. „Da merkst du genau, wie dein Schiff im Wasser liegt. Wenn das Schiff voll und steif ist, bewegt es sich in den Wellen wie ein Stehaufmännchen.“ Außer ein paar kleineren Verletzungen ist Fiedler allerdings nie etwas Schlimmeres passiert. Wirklich nicht? „Oh, doch!“, fällt ihm lachend ein: „Ich habe mal vier Container verloren im Hafen von Norfolk. Die hat mir ein Kranfahrer vom Schiff geschoben.“

Kapitän ist einer der wenigen Berufe, wo du im Alter immer besser wirst

Seine Jahre bei Hapag-Lloyd seien seine besten, findet der Kapitän, auch wenn sich durch Corona einiges verändert hat. Es gibt wenige Dinge an der Seefahrt, die ihn stören. Dazu gehören die unzähligen behördlichen Vorschriften weltweit: „An Bord gilt Mülltrennung, was wir natürlich beherzigen. In China haben sie uns dann aber so lange durchsucht, bis sie einen kleinen Plastikdeckel im Papierkorb im Maschinenraum gefunden haben, das hat uns eine Bemängelung eingebracht, obwohl die Jungs im Hafen den ganzen getrennten Müll wieder zusammenschütten.“ Oder in Südafrika: „Da habe die Behörden so lange gewühlt, bis sie ein paar Bierflaschen bei der Mannschaft gefunden haben. 150 Dollar Strafe pro Person, das ist doch Wahnsinn!“ Uwe Fiedler führt diese Entwicklung auch auf 9/11 zurück: „Seitdem ist alles viel restriktiver geworden.“

based on gut instinct, and I don't need to think about them." His experience has also taught him that speed isn't everything – especially in stormy weather. "I'd rather be late and safe than punctual and battered," Fiedler adds. Nevertheless, he has had to take his vessels through the odd storm from time to time – such as on the Tasman Sea between Australia and Tasmania, where the Pacific and Indian oceans meet and waves are extremely high. "You realise exactly how your ship is lying in the water. If your vessel is full and stiff, it moves in the waves like a roly-poly toy." Aside from a couple minor injuries, Fiedler has still always come out unscathed. Really? "Oh, wait!" he says with a smile. "I did lose four containers in the Port of Norfolk. A crane operator knocked them off the vessel."

Even if the pandemic has changed a few things, the years he has worked for Hapag-Lloyd have been his best, the captain says. In fact, there are only a few things about seafaring that he doesn't like. This includes the countless official regulations around the world. "There is garbage separation on board, which of course we take seriously. But, in China, they searched us until they eventually found a small plastic lid in the trash can in the engine room, which resulted in a reprimand, even though the guys in the port were just throwing all the separated garbage back together again anyway." Or take an example from South Africa: "The authorities kept poking around until they found a few beer bottles on the crew. Each of them received a $150 fine, which is just insane!" Fiedler thinks that 9/11 is one of the reasons behind this trend, saying that, "Everything has gotten a lot more restrictive since then."

Die Wehmut fährt mit: Im Oktober 2022 verlässt Uwe Fiedler sein letztes Schiff, die „New York Express“ in Panama

Already nostalgic: In October 2022, Uwe Fiedler leaves his last ship, the "New York Express", in Panama.

>>

Kanu statt großer Pott, Chips futtern mit der Tochter

Abenteuer und Entspannung gleichermaßen sucht der sportliche Kapitän auf seinen unzähligen Reisen: Ob er allein mit dem Kanu den Yukon River hinunterpaddelt (Jack Londons „Lockruf des Goldes" war Inspiration), 1.500 Kilometer mit dem Kajak entlang der grönländischen Küste zurücklegt oder mit seiner Frau – von Beruf Schiffsmaklerin – in Skandinavien unterwegs ist. „Norwegen und Schweden begeistern uns besonders. Nicht zufällig heißt unsere Tochter Svea". Und auch wenn er es nicht an die große Glocke hängen mag: Svea fuhr bis letztes Jahr ebenfalls für Hapag-Lloyd zur See – als Erste Offizierin. „Auf der ‚Kuala Lumpur' sind wir während ihrer Ausbildungszeit sogar mal zusammengefahren. Tagsüber war ich ihr strenger Kapitän und abends hat sie mir dann auf dem Sofa die Chips weggefuttert", lacht Uwe Fiedler. Dass sich die Zwei mal auf ein Stündchen zum Kaffee in Hongkong verabredeten, als ihre Schiffe im selben Hafen lagen, passt zum Lebensgefühl der Familie. Oder wie Uwe Fiedler es sagt: „Wer so aufwächst wie wir, kann nicht Finanzbeamter werden." Vom Leben auf See erzählen seine Bilder auf den folgenden Seiten.

Canoe instead of big boat, eating chips with his daughter

On his countless voyages, the captain has always sought to strike a good balance between adventure and relaxation – whether he paddles down the Yukon River alone in a canoe (after being inspired by Jack London's novel "Burning Daylight"), kayaks 1,500 kilometres along the coast of Greenland, or travels through Scandinavia with his wife, a shipbroker by trade. "We are particularly big fans of Norway and Sweden. It's no coincidence that our daughter's name is Svea." And even if he doesn't want to shout it from the rooftops, Svea is also sailing for Hapag-Lloyd these days – as a chief officer.

"We even sailed together once on the 'Kuala Lumpur' while she was in her training period. During the day, I was her strict captain and, in the evening, she scarfed down all my chips on the sofa," Fiedler says with a laugh. The fact that the two of them arrange to spend an hour together over coffee in Hong Kong when their ships are in the same port fits in with the family's philosophy of life. Or, as Fiedler puts it: "If you've grown up like us, you can't become a tax inspector." His pictures on the following pages tell of life at sea.

Was macht Uwe Fiedler heute?

Feierabend! Seit Kurzem ist der engagierte Kapitän in Rente und kümmert sich um Haus, Garten und um seinen ersten Enkel. „Die letzten Fahrten waren herausfordernd und ich bin ganz froh, dass jetzt Schluss ist!", erzählt er. Trotzdem ließ er es sich nicht nehmen, zum Abschluss noch den Sportraum der „New York Express" zu verschönern. Uwe Fiedler besorgte sich in New York Laminat, Lichtspots und Fototapete und nutzt die lange Zeit auf der Pazifiküberfahrt nach Asien für den Ausbau. Von seinem handwerklichen Geschick wird in Zukunft Enkel Carl Fiete profitieren, das Baumhaus in der alten Hauseiche ist bereits geplant. Uwe Fiedlers Tochter Svea hat ihre Elternzeit ein Jahr nach Geburt beendet und arbeitet Vollzeit als „Central Planner" für Hapag-Lloyd – was auch prima im Homeoffice funktioniert.

What's Uwe Fiedler doing today?

Relaxing! The hard-working captain recently retired and is now taking care of his house, garden and first grandchild. "The last few voyages were quite challenging, and I'm happy that it's over now!" he admits. But before disembarking from the "New York Express" for the last time, he still took time to have its sports room renovated. Fiedler got laminate, spot lighting fixtures and photo wallpaper in New York and then used the long crossing of the Pacific to Asia to make the improvements. His grandson, Carl Fiete, will also benefit from his handicraft skills one day – as there are already plans to build a tree house in the old oak tree. Fiedler's daughter, Svea, finished her parental leave one year after giving birth and now works full-time as a central planner for Hapag-Lloyd – which she can also do just fine from the home office.

NYK LOGISTICS
tex
OOCL
TAL
OOCL
APL
TAL

HAMBURG SÜD
CMA CGM
Hapag-Lloyd
CSAV
UASC
EVERGREEN
COSCO

HYUNDAI

Mit allen Stürmen gewaschen

Udo Domke

Seen it all on the high seas

Udo Domke sollte die Apotheke seiner Mutter übernehmen. Aber mit dem Umzug nach Hamburg und der Nähe zum Hafen kam es anders. Ein Gespräch über 42 Jahre Seefahrt mit Wettern aller Art, spannenden Forschungsreisen und wie er dem Erdbeben 2011 in Tokio entging.

Udo Domke was supposed to take over his mother's pharmacy. But things turned out differently after he moved to a location in Hamburg near the port. A conversation about 42 years of seafaring through all kinds of weather, exciting research trips, and how he escaped the 2011 earthquake in Tokyo.

Beim Rundgang durch das Leercontainerdepot berichtet Udo Domke von seine Jahrzehnten auf See

Domke talks about his decades at sea during a walk through the CMR empty container depot

<<

Pharmazie studieren und irgendwann Pillen drehen – das interessierte mich einfach nicht!", erzählt Kapitän Udo Domke bei einem Spaziergang durch das Leercontainerdepot CMR in Hamburg-Wilhelmsburg. Er erinnert sich noch gut an seine Kindheit in Helmstedt, die Apotheke seiner Mutter, in der er als kleiner Junge im Hinterzimmer spielte. Seine Eltern hatten sich gewünscht, dass ihr ältester Sohn die Apotheke übernimmt. Dann zog die Familie für einen neuen Job des Vaters nach Hamburg. „Und als ich hier mit 17 zufällig einen Ersten Offizier kennenlernte, dachte ich: Ein vielseitiger Beruf – das könnte es sein."

Nach seiner Internatszeit in Bad Sachsa und Plön, in der er bereits „erste Erfahrungen in Sachen Großfamilie" sammelte, bewarb sich der Abiturient bei Hapag-Lloyd, machte eine Ausbildung zum Nautischen Offizier und erlebte das erste schwere Wetter auf der „MS Friesenstein" 1979: „Nachts um drei erwischten

Studying pharmacology and making pills at some point – that just didn't interest me at all!" says Captain Udo Domke during a walk through the CMR empty container depot in the Wilhelmsburg quarter of Hamburg. He still remembers well his childhood in the central-northern German town of Helmstedt and his mother's pharmacy, where he played as a small boy in the back room. His parents had wanted their oldest son to take over the pharmacy. But then the family moved to Hamburg after his father got a new job there. "And when I met a chief mate here by chance when I was 17 years old, I thought to myself: 'A job that offers a lot of diversity– that could be the one for me.'"

After his boarding-school years in Bad Sachsa and Plön, during which he already gained some "initial experience in

wir mitten auf dem Atlantik die Ausläufer des Hurrikans „Floyd". Der Stülcken-80t Schwergutbaum des Frachters hatte sich losgerissen und wir versuchten von allen Seiten, Leinen über den Haken zu werfen, um das Ding wieder einzufangen." So ein Haken bewege sich in Sturm und Dünung wie ein wild gewordener Stier, berichtet Udo Domke: „Wenn der einmal richtig durchgeschwungen wäre, er hätte die ganze Brücke zerstört." Mit vereinten Kräften bändigte die Mannschaft den „Stier" schließlich: „Egal welcher Dienstgrad, alle haben mitgeholfen, sonst hätten wir das nicht gepackt."

Unterwegs auf allem, was schwimmt

Nach dem Studium zum Wirtschaftsingenieur für Seeverkehr hatte Hapag-Lloyd zwar keine passende Stelle für den 29-Jährigen. „Aber ich konnte bei der Reederei F. Laeisz anfangen und Ferdinand Laeisz hatte 1847 die HAPAG immerhin mitgegründet", so Udo Domke: „Fruchtschifffahrt, Bulkschifffahrt, Containerschifffahrt – ich bin dann alles gefahren, was schwimmt", erzählt er gut gelaunt. Heute noch kann er fachmännisch über Reifeprozesse und Transport von Bananen, Kiwi und Co. referieren, weiß über Kühlgrade und die richtige Lagerung Bescheid: „Mit einem einzigen Apfel kannst du eine ganze Bananenladung ruinieren."

Schwere See vor der Dominikanischen Republik und ein spannender Ausflug in die Polarforschung

1995 erhielt er das Kapitänspatent und konnte seine Erfahrung schnell unter Beweis stellen. Sein Kühlschiff lag in der Bucht von Manzanillo, der Nordküste der Dominikanische Republik nahe des Rio de Massacre, als eine Kaltfront aufzog. „Wir hatten an der Bananenpier festgemacht, sieben Meter Ladetiefe, damit die Pflanzer

big-family matters", the high school graduate applied to Hapag-Lloyd and trained to become a nautical officer. His first encounter with severe weather came in 1979 on board the "MS Friesenstein". "We were hit by the remnants of Hurricane Floyd at 3 o'clock in the morning on the Atlantic. The cargo ship's 80-tonne Stülcken heavy lift derrick had broken loose, and we tried from all sides to throw lines over the hook to secure it." In a storm and swell, Domke continues, a hook like that jumps around like a bull gone wild. "If it had really swung the wrong way at full force, it would have destroyed the entire bridge." By coordinating their efforts, the crew finally managed to "tame the bull". "Everyone pitched in no matter their rank – or we wouldn't have pulled it off," he adds.

You can ruin an entire shipment of bananas with a single apple

At sea on everything that floats

When the 29-year-old finished his studies to become an industrial engineer for maritime transport, Hapag-Lloyd didn't have a suitable open position for him. "But I was able to get my start at the shipping company F. Laeisz, whose founder, Ferdinand Laeisz, had in any case also been one of the co-founders of HAPAG in 1847," Domke recounts. "Fruit shipping, bulk shipping, container shipping – I then sailed everything that floats," he says cheerfully. Even today, he can give expert lectures on the ripening process and transport of bananas, kiwis and the like, and knows about the proper refrigeration degrees and storage methods. "You can ruin an entire shipment of bananas with a single apple," he adds.

gut anliefern können. 25 Knoten waren vorausgesagt, aber dann kam die Front mit 55 Knoten direkt auf uns zu. Sämtliche Leinen brachen und ich musste aufpassen, dass ich nicht mit dem Marineschiff direkt vor uns kollidierte. Der Sturm drückte unser Heck von der Pier. Ich versuchte noch mit dem Hieven des Ankers den Steven von der Pier abzubringen, aber das Schiff schlug quer und kam auf Grund an der steil aufsteigenden vulkanischen Küste. Der Leitende Ingenieur sagte nur: ‚Fahr los!' und ich fuhr. Haarscharf steuerten wir mit schleifendem Anker an der Fingerpier vorbei raus in die Bucht. Dort haben wir abgewettert, bis alles vorbei war."

Schon ein einziger Apfel kann eine ganze Bananenladung ruinieren

Im November 2001 brach Domke zu neuen Ufern auf und wurde auf der „Polarstern" eingesetzt, einem staatlichen Forschungseisbrecher des Alfred-Wegener-Instituts für Polar- und Meeresforschung (AWI) in Bremerhaven. „Einen Eisbrecher mit vier Maschinen und 20.000 PS zu steuern, unterwegs mit zig Wissenschaftlerinnen und Wissenschaftlern zu sein, das ist schon besonders", schwärmt der Kapitän.

Trotz seiner Erfahrung fing er hier quasi von vorn an: „Eisbrecher und Eis verhalten sich komplett anders als Frachter und Meer: Die kinetische Energie schiebt den Brecher auf die Scholle, durch das Eigengewicht des Schiffes bricht das Eis an der dünnsten Stelle und dort fährst du dann weiter. Dafür gibt's keine Ausbildung, das lernt man erst an Bord." Umweltschutz und Klimawandel interessieren ihn seither besonders. „Einmal vor der irischen Küste haben unsere Forscher

Rough seas off the Dominican Republic and an exciting foray into polar research

After earning his master's certificate in 1995, Domke was quickly able to demonstrate the skills he had acquired over time. His refrigerated ship was in Manzanillo Bay, on the northern coast of the Dominican Republic near the Dajabón River, when a cold front moved in. "We had moored at the banana pier, and the ship's seven-metre loading depth meant the growers could really pile in a lot of fruit. The forecast had predicted winds of 25 knots, but then the front came right at us at 55 knots. All the mooring lines snapped, and I had to be careful not to collide with the navy ship right in front of us. The storm pushed our stern away from the pier. I tried to get the bow off the pier by heaving the anchor, but the ship turned perpendicular and ran aground on the rugged volcanic coast. Then the chief engineer just said 'Go!' and I gave the ship power. We then steered the vessel by a hair's breadth past the finger pier and out into the bay while dragging our anchor the entire time. Then we weathered the storm there until it was all over."

In November 2001, Domke set out for new horizons and was assigned to work on the "Polarstern", a government-owned research icebreaker operated by the Bremerhaven-based Alfred Wegener Institute for Polar and Marine Research (AWI). "To navigate an icebreaker with four engines and to be out at sea with countless scientists – that was really something special," the captain says with enthusiasm.

Despite his years of experience, the new position was practically like starting from zero. "Icebreakers and ice behave in a completely different way than cargo ships and the open sea: The kinetic energy

Containerboxen statt Pillendosen: Udo Domke wehrte sich erfolgreich gegen den Wunsch seiner Eltern, Apotheker zu werden

Container boxes instead of pillboxes: Domke successfully resisted his parents' desire for him to become a pharmacist

>>

Hapag-Lloyd
Hapag-Lloyd
Hapag-Lloyd
Hapag-Lloyd

Würde er gern noch mal losfahren? Nicht nötig, findet der Kapitän a. D., er habe die Seefahrt von den schönsten Seiten kennengelernt

Would he ever like to go back to sea? The retired captain says there's no need, as he has already experienced all the best aspects of seafaring

gefilmt, was am Meeresboden übrig bleibt, wenn große Trawler mit ihren Schleppnetzen drüberfahren: absolut nichts!" Udo Domke ist froh, dass genau diese Ecke vor der irischen Küste, am Stachelschwein Rücken (engl. Porcupine Bank), heute unter Schutz steht: „Jetzt wird da nur noch mit Leinen und Haken geangelt."

Zurück zu den Wurzeln

Knapp 30 Jahre nach seiner Ausbildung und mit jeder Menge Expertise im Gepäck, kehrte der damals 50-jährige Kapitän zu seinem ehemaligen Ausbilder

of the icebreaker propels it onto the floe. Then the ship's own weight causes the ice to break at the thinnest point, and that's where you keep sailing forward. There isn't any training for that; you can only learn it on board."

Since then, Domke has had a keen interest in issues related to environmental protection and climate change. "Off the coast of Ireland, our researchers once filmed what is left of the seabed after big trawlers sail over it with their dragnets: absolutely nothing!" Domke is glad that exactly this area off the western coast of

zurück: „Das war wie nach Hause kommen!“ Der Enthusiasmus jedes einzelnen Mitarbeiters, die Leute, das Arbeitsklima: „Man spürt einfach, dass hier auch in der Führungsetage echte Seefahrer unterwegs sind.“ Es folgten fünf Jahre auf der „Frankfurt Express“. Immer wieder fuhr er seine Lieblingsroute über den Pazifik: „Da hat man manchmal rund zehn Tage auf See, keine Häfen, stattdessen alle Schattierungen des Meeres. Das beeindruckt mich noch immer. Weil einem bewusst wird, wie unbedeutend der einzelne Mensch angesichts dieser überwältigenden Natur ist.“

Was er an Hapag-Lloyd besonders schätzt, ist der Umgang mit dem Personal. Nie werde er vergessen, wie sich Flottenchef Richard von Berlepsch kümmerte, als Domke mit der „Dresden Express“ das Tohoku-Erdbeben 2011 erlebte: „Wir liefen gerade mit dem Lotsen in den Hafen von Tokio ein, als es losging. Es kam kein Alarm, nichts, einfach nur eine merkwürdige Schwingung im Schiff. Der Lotse an Bord telefonierte, einzig das Wort: ‚Erdbeben‘ kam aus seinem Mund. Die Containerbrücken vor uns an der Pier gerieten derart ins Schwanken, dass ein plötzliches Kollabieren nahelag.“ Kapitän und Mannschaft legten im Eiltempo ab und gingen weit vor Tokio vor Anker. „Mittlerweile hatten wir auch erfahren, dass Fukushima betroffen war. Die radioaktive Wolke zog anfangs nach Nord-Ost raus aufs Meer, bevor sie am 14. März in unsere Richtung unterwegs war. Wir hatten zwar ein Messgerät an Bord und die Werte waren noch unbedenklich. Aber würde das auch so bleiben? Richard von Berlepsch stand seit dem Erdbeben mit dem Bundesamt für Strahlenschutz in Verbindung. Dann kam der Anruf: ‚Ihr lauft aus und geht nicht an die Pier!‘ Nach dem Hauptbeben gab es weitere Nachbeben, ginge das Schiff an die Pier, könnte ein umstürzender Kran

Ireland, on the Porcupine Bank, has been placed under protection. “Now it’s just line-and-hook fishing there,” he notes.

Back to his roots

The safety of the people on board has always been the top priority

Almost 30 years after his training and with a lot of expertise under his belt, the then-50-year-old captain returned to his former instructor. “It was like a homecoming!” he says. He then lists off the people, the working atmosphere and how every single employee is enthusiastic, adding that: “You simply get the feeling that genuine seafarers are at work there, including at the management level.”

He then spent five years on the “Frankfurt Express”, on which he repeatedly sailed on his favourite route across the Pacific. “You sometimes have about 10 days at sea on this route without any ports, but instead with all the shades of the sea. That still impresses me, as you realise just how insignificant individual humans are in the face of overpowering nature.”

When asked what he especially appreciates about Hapag-Lloyd, he says it is the way it treats its employees. He will never forget how Richard von Berlepsch, the head of Fleet Management, took care of him and the “Dresden Express” when the Tohoku earthquake struck Japan in 2011. “We were just entering the port of Tokyo with the pilot when it started,” he recounts. “There wasn’t any alarm, nothing, just a strange vibration in the ship. The pilot on board made a phone call, and only one word came out of his mouth: ‘Earthquake’. The container gantry cranes in front of us on the pier started to vibrate so much that a sudden collapse was imminent.” The captain and crew sailed away

das Schiff unter sich festsetzen." Das sei typisch Hapag-Lloyd: „Die Sicherheit der Menschen an Bord geht immer vor."

Die Sicherheit der Menschen an Bord geht bei Hapag-Lloyd immer vor

Wohlbehalten brachte der Kapitän Mannschaft und Schiff zurück nach Hamburg. Hier endete nach 42 Jahren auch die berufliche Reise für Udo Domke: „Irgendwann ist es auch mal gut, ich habe ja alles erlebt", resümiert er. Keine Ambitionen, bei Hapag-Lloyd noch mal mitzumischen? Udo Domke schüttelt den Kopf: „Ich kann gut loslassen. Aber wenn jemand noch ein bisschen von meinen Erfahrungen hören will, soll er sich gern melden!", lacht der Kapitän a. D. und gibt zum Schluss einen Lesetipp: „Barrow's Boys", ein Buch von Fergus Fleming über Expeditionen ehemaliger britischer Marineoffiziere und ihrer Mannschaften im 19. Jahrhundert, das er auf seiner letzten Reise gelesen hat. Den Seeleuten darin ergeht es weit weniger gut als Kapitän Domke: „Alle Expeditionen scheiterten und waren so ziemlich das Gegenteil von dem, was die britische Krone als Entdeckernation zu feiern vorgab. Alles wahr und absolut packend erzählt!"

from land as fast as they could and anchored far off Tokyo.

"By then, we had also learned that Fukushima had been impacted," he continues. "The radioactive cloud initially drifted out to sea in a north-easterly direction before moving towards us on 14 March. We had a radiation measuring device on board, and the readings were still harmless. But would things stay that way, too? Since the earthquake happened, Richard von Berlepsch had been in constant contact with Germany's Federal Office for Radiation Protection. Then the call came: 'Put out to sea, and don't go to the pier!'" That was typical Hapag-Lloyd, he says, noting that: "The safety of the people on board has always been the top priority." The captain then brought both the crew and ship safely back to Hamburg. Domke's long career also ended there after 42 years. "That's good at a certain point, as I've already seen it all," he concludes. When asked if he ever feels any ambitions to rejoin Hapag-Lloyd, the freshly minted pensioner shakes his head and says: "I can let go easily. But if anyone wants to hear a bit more about my experiences, please feel free to contact me!"

His reading tip: Fergus Flemings book "Barrow's Boys: The Original Extreme Adventures", which Captain Domke read on his final voyage. The book is about the perilous journeys to uncharted areas that British naval officers and their crews made in the 19th century. "All of their expeditions were failures and pretty much the exact opposite of what the British Crown claimed while celebrating itself as a nation of explorers," Domke says. "And it's all true and absolutely thrillingly recounted!"

Was macht Udo Domke heute?

Udo Domke und seine Frau haben mit dem Golfspielen angefangen und arbeiten fleißig an ihren Handicaps. Außerdem engagiert sich der 65-Jährige ehrenamtlich im Internationalen Maritimen Museum Hamburg, gibt dort mit vielen Kollegen, auch von Hapag-Lloyd, Simulatorfahrten.

What's Udo Domke doing today?

Domke and his wife have taken up golf and are working diligently on their handicap. The 65-year-old is also involved in the the International Maritime Museum Hamburg, where, where he conducts simulator rides also with many colleagues from Hapag-Lloyd.

Hapag-Lloyd
snch
Certified
STEEL FLOOR
SUPER
HEAVY
TIR
PLATE
INSIDE
REPAIR WITH
"CORTEN"
STEEL ONLY
APPROVED FOR TRANSPORT
UNDER CUSTOMS SEAL
CSC SAFETY APPROVAL

Zwischen Kapitänspatent und Wickelkommode

Immanuel Jürgens

Between master's license and nappy-changing table

Mit gerade mal 35 Jahren wurde Immanuel Jürgens Kapitän. Der Mann, der eigentlich Medizin studieren wollte, kann sich heute nichts Besseres vorstellen, als zur See zu fahren. Hier erzählt er, was man aus Fehlern lernen kann, wie er beherzt einen verletzten Unterarm versorgte, und warum er auch gern an der Wickelkommode statt auf der Brücke steht.

Immanuel Jürgens became a captain when he was only 35 years old. Although he actually wanted to study medicine, now he can't imagine anything better than a life at sea. Here, he tells us what we can learn from mistakes, how he courageously treated an injured forearm, and why he is now also happy to stand at the nappy-changing table instead of on the bridge.

Eine funkende Seenot-Boje brachte den damaligen Chief Mate in Bedrängnis – seiner Ernennung zum Kapitän tat das keinen Abbruch

An activated distress buoy caused the then-chief mate some trouble – but this didn't affect his appointment to captain

<<

Wenn ich eines nicht noch mal mache, dann eine Seenot-Boje im Müll zu entsorgen", erzählt Immanuel Jürgens und grinst. Der Vorfall ereignete sich auf der „Hamburg Express", als er vor einigen Jahren den Sicherheitsstore in chinesischen Gewässern aufräumen ließ. Damals war er noch Chief Mate. „Die Boje stand in der Ecke und ich dachte, das alte Ding kann jetzt doch auch mal weg. Wir gaben sie in Yantian zusammen mit unserem Müll ab und fuhren weiter. Zehn Stunden später plötzlich ein aufgeregter Anruf aus Hamburg: ‚Wir kriegen hier Notsignale, was ist passiert?' Der Kapitän war irritiert, denn bei uns an Bord war alles in Ordnung." Immanuel Jürgens schwante, dass das womöglich mit der entsorgten Boje zu tun haben könnte. „Tatsächlich hatte ein Müllmann irgendwo in Südchina das Notsignal ausgelöst, und das funkte munter von der Müllkippe an die deutsche Seenotrettung, die dann sofort Hapag-Lloyd kontaktiert hatte."

If there's one thing I won't do again, it's to throw a distress buoy in the rubbish," Immanuel Jürgens says with a grin. The incident occurred a few years ago on the "Hamburg Express" when he was having the safety store – meaning the storage room for the fire-fighting equipment – cleaned up in Chinese waters. At the time, he was still a chief mate. "The buoy was sitting in the corner, and I thought that the old thing could go now," he recounts. "We dropped it off in Yantian along with our rubbish and sailed on. Ten hours later, we received an alarmed call from Hamburg, saying: 'We're getting distress signals here! What happened?' The captain was puzzled because everything was in order on board."

Then it occurred to Jürgens that this might have something to do with the buoy they had gotten rid of. "And, in fact,

Immanuel Jürgens beichtete zerknirscht das Malheur. „Glücklicherweise war der Kapitän gnädig und der Vorfall nach zwei Tagen vergessen. So ist es eben: Wenn du Entscheidungen triffst, können dir auch Fehler unterlaufen." Viele Fehler können es bei dem gebürtigen Reinbeker nicht gewesen sein, denn seine Ernennung zum Kapitän erhielt er mitten in der Pandemie 2020 mit gerade mal 35 Jahren.

Vom Krankenhaus aufs Containerschiff

Dabei wollte Immanuel Jürgens eigentlich Arzt werden „Ich interessierte mich für Medizin, hatte nach Schule und Bundeswehr zwei Praktika im Krankenhaus absolviert. Als ich keinen Studienplatz bekam, überlegte ich, was noch möglich wäre und kam mit einem befreundeten Schifffahrtskaufmann ins Gespräch. Das hörte sich spannend an – nur im Büro zu sitzen, das konnte ich mir nicht vorstellen. Mit dem Schiff die weite Welt erkunden, das klang schon besser!" So bewarb sich Immanuel Jürgens 2006 zur Ausbildung als Schiffsmechaniker bei Hapag-Lloyd. Und fiel erst mal durch. „Ich habe wohl einen nicht sonderlich technisch interessierten Eindruck gemacht. Allerdings bekam ich zwei Wochen vor Ausbildungsbeginn das Angebot, als Nautischer Offiziersanwärter anzufangen." So betrat der damals 22-Jährige als Auszubildender mit sieben weiteren NOAs das erste Mal im Leben ein Containerschiff, die „Chicago Express", die 2006 neu als Ausbildungsschiff startete. „Zehn Wochen geballtes Wissen einatmen, das Schiff vom Rumpf bis zur Brücke kennenlernen, die ersten Wachen schieben und dazu ein paar großartige Landgänge von Rotterdam bis Singapur – das war anstrengend, aufregend und schön zugleich!", berichtet der Kapitän rückblickend. Dass zur Seefahrt auch der eine oder andere Sturm gehört,

a dustman somewhere in southern China had triggered the distress signal, and this cheerfully chirped from the rubbish heap all the way to the German Maritime Search and Rescue Service, which then immediately contacted Hapag-Lloyd." With remorse, Jürgens admitted to his slip-up. "The captain was fortunately forgiving, and the incident was forgotten after a few days. That's just how it is: When you make decisions, you can also make mistakes." In any case, the native of Reinbek – a town just a short drive east of Hamburg – couldn't have made very many mistakes, as he was promoted to captain in the middle of the pandemic in 2020 at the young age of 35.

Blackout, complete shutdown. And the wind force was between nine and 10

From the hospital to the container ship

Jürgens actually wanted to become a physician. "I was interested in medicine, and I had completed two internships at hospitals after finishing school and my military service. When I didn't get a place at university, I thought about what else I could do and got into a conversation with a friend who was a shipping agent. It sounded exciting – but I couldn't imagine myself only sitting in an office. But exploring the vast world by ship? Now that sounded a lot better!"

So, in 2006, Jürgens submitted an application to Hapag-Lloyd for an apprenticeship to qualify as a ship mechanic. But he wasn't accepted at first. "I guess I didn't give off the impression of being very interested in technical matters. But two weeks

erlebte Immanuel Jürgens auf seiner zweiten Reise als Auszubildender: „Das war im Nordatlantik vor Halifax. Wir mussten durch ein Sturmtief, das Schiff rollte wie wild. Wir saßen in der Messe, als das Schiff plötzlich so überholte, dass die Stühle am Tisch umfielen. Ein mitreisender Techniker stand aus Reflex auf und wurde beinahe an die Wand geschleudert. Glücklicherweise ist ihm nichts Schlimmes passiert.

Blackout, totaler Stillstand. Und das bei neun bis zehn Windstärken

Erste Hilfe am Unterarm, aber bloß nicht zu viel Druck!

Wie sich Verantwortung anfühlt, erlebte Immanuel Jürgens als Chief Mate auf der „New York Express“. „Wir lagen im Hafen von Mersin an der türkischen Küste. Während der Reise hatten wir das Schiff für einen Scrubber-Umbau vorbereitet, also für ein neues Abgasreinigungssystem, das in der Hamburg-Klasse getestet werden sollte. Dazu mussten wir im Maschinenraum einiges umbauen, die nebenan liegenden Kabinen entkernen und das Material an Land entsorgen. Am Kai stand ein Truck mit unserem Matrosen auf der Ladefläche, der unter anderen auch scharfkantige Metallplatten entgegennehmen musste. Da passierte es: Er verletzte sich an einer der Kanten, schnitt sich ziemlich heftig den Unterarm auf. Ich war gerade im Büro, als mich der aufgeregte Funkspruch erreichte. Einen Krankenwagen rufen? Selbst Hand anlegen? Der Zweite Wachoffizier und ich entschieden dann, den Arm zu versorgen, sprich, wir tackerten die offenen Wunde. Glücklicherweise war der Mann hart im Nehmen und die Situation nicht lebensbedrohlich. So fuhr

before the apprenticeship was supposed to begin, I received an offer to start out as a deck cadet." Thus, as one of eight nautical apprentices, the then-22-year-old boarded a container ship for the first time in his life. It was the "Chicago Express", which has been a Hapag-Lloyd training vessel since it was commissioned in 2006.

"Breathing in loads of information for 10 weeks, familiarising myself with the ship from hull to bridge, standing my first watches, plus some great shore leaves from Rotterdam to Singapore – it was exhausting, exciting and beautiful all at the same time!" the captain fondly recalls.

On his second voyage as a cadet, Jürgens learned first-hand that seafaring also involves weathering the occasional storm. "That was on the North Atlantic off Halifax," he recounts. "We had to go through a storm depression, and the ship was rolling like crazy. We were sitting in the mess room when suddenly the ship heeled in such a way that the chairs at the table fell over. A technician travelling with us stood up out of reflex – and was almost thrown against the wall. Luckily, nothing bad happened to him."

First aid on a forearm – just don't put too much pressure on it!

Jürgens got his first taste of what responsibility feels like as a chief mate on board the "New York Express". "We were berthed in the Port of Mersin on the southern coast of Turkish. During the voyage, we had prepared the ship to be retrofitted with a scrubber – meaning a new exhaust gas cleaning system – which was supposed to be tested on a Hamburg-class vessel. To do this, we had to rearrange some things in the engine room, empty out the adjacent cabins, and dispose of the material

Auf der „New York Express“ bewies Kapitän Jürgens medizinisches Geschick: Fachmännisch tackerte er den verletzten Unterarm eines Matrosen

Captain Jürgens demonstrated his medical knowledge on the "New York Express": He expertly stapled the injured forearm of a seafarer

>>

der Verletzte noch drei Wochen mit und ging erst in Singapur von Bord“, erzählt der Kapitän und wiegelt ab: „Sicherlich gibt es dramatischere Situationen, die wir an Bord meistern müssen, doch auch im Alltag zeigt sich, was jeder Einzelne draufhat.“

Zwei Jahre ist er jetzt schon Kapitän: „Aber jede Reise ist neu und anders – das mag ich so an der Seefahrt.“

He has already been a captain for two years: "But every voyage is new and different – and that's what I like about seafaring."

An seinem Arbeitgeber schätzt Immanuel Jürgens besonders den Umgang mit den Mitarbeitenden. „Hapag-Lloyd kümmert sich um seine Leute und wertschätzt jeden Einzelnen. Auch das Weiterbildungsangebot finde ich beeindruckend, man hat das Gefühl, dass in die eigenen Leute gern investiert wird. Und das macht am Ende den guten Spirit aus, der bei uns herrscht.“ Als Kapitän spürt Immanuel Jürgens, dass auch er an Bord maßgeblich für die Stimmung der Besatzung verantwortlich ist. „Mal abgesehen vom Koch“, lacht er und fährt fort: „Ein gutes Klima schaffen, nicht unnötig Druck aufbauen, den Leuten vertrauen – das finde ich wichtig. Erst wenn es hart auf hart kommt, merkst du, ob du auf die Menschen zählen kannst.

Wenn sich die Maschine plötzlich abschaltet…

Seine erste Kapitänsfahrt im August 2020 von Genua über den Atlantik und zurück verlief reibungslos. „Die Einarbeitung war super, alles erfahrene Leute an Bord, ein guter Start!“ Aber schon auf der zweiten Rundreise musste Immanuel Jürgens beweisen, dass er auch mit Stress umgehen kann: „Wir kamen aus Savannah, gut drei Stunden auf dem Savannah River Richtung Nordatlantik lagen hinter uns. Gerade hatten wir den Lotsen verabschie-

on land. On the quay, there was a truck with one of our ordinary seamen on the loading platform, who had to receive a number of things, including some metal plates with sharp edges. That's when it happened: He hurt himself on one of the edges, cutting his forearm pretty badly. I had just arrived in the office when the excited radio message reached me. Should I call an ambulance? Or should I try to perform first aid myself? Then the second officer of the watch and I decided to treat the arm by stapling the open wound shut. Luckily, the seaman was a tough guy, and the situation wasn't life-threatening. The injured man sailed with us for another three weeks and only disembarked in Singapore," says the captain, before modestly adding: "There are definitely some even more dramatic situations that we have to deal with on board, but everyday life also shows what every individual is capable of."

What Jürgens particularly appreciates about his employer is the way it treats its employees. "Hapag-Lloyd takes care of its people and values each individual. I also find the continuing-education offers impressive, as you really get the feeling that they are keen to invest in their own people. And, in the end, that's also what fosters the high spirits that we enjoy." As captain, Jürgens feels that he is largely responsible for the spirits of the crew on board. "Apart from the cook," he adds with a laugh before noting: "Creating a good atmosphere, not building up any unnecessary pressure, trusting people – that's what I think is important. It's only when the going gets tough that you learn whether you can really count on people."

When the engine suddenly shuts down…

Jürgens had his first voyage as a captain in August 2020. It was from Genoa across the Atlantic and back – and everything went

det, um aufs offene Meer zu fahren. Da schaltete sich plötzlich die Maschine ab. Blackout, totaler Stillstand. Und das bei neun bis zehn Windstärken". Eine Hydraulikleitung war geplatzt. „Wir ankerten und riefen alle verfügbaren Leute zur Reparatur der Leitung und zum Reinigen des Maschinenraums. Begeisterung sieht an einem Sonntagmittag anders aus, aber die gemeinsame Arbeit, das Reinigen und Reparieren der Maschine hat alle zusammengeschweißt – letztendlich war das ein super Manöver."

Vaterfreuden!

Mit solchen Abenteuern war zwischendrin Schluss, denn als junger Vater entschied sich Immanuel Jürgens für eine dreimonatige Elternzeit. Rechtzeitig zur Geburt kam er nach Hamburg und freute sich, für Tochter Jonna und Freundin Stella da zu sein. „Die Geburt von Jonna ist das Schönste, was ich bisher erlebt habe, einfach ein unglaubliches Gefühl!", freut sich Immanuel Jürgens. „Und ich habe ein gutes Gefühl mit meinem Arbeitgeber. Die Seefahrt mag nicht immer familienfreundlich sein, aber Hapag-Lloyd ist es auf jeden Fall!"

smoothly. "The onboarding was great, and all the people on board were experienced," he says. "So I got off to a good start!"

But already on the second round voyage, Jürgens had to prove that he can also handle stress. "We were coming from Savannah, and we had already been sailing on the Savannah River towards the North Atlantic for more than three hours. We had just said goodbye to the pilot and were heading towards the open sea. Then the engine suddenly went quiet. Blackout, complete shutdown. And, to make matters worse, the wind force was between nine and 10 [editor's note: between "strong/severe gale" and "storm/whole gale" on the Beaufort scale]. A hydraulic line had ruptured. We dropped anchor and called everyone available to repair the pipe and clean up the engine room. It wasn't the kind of thing you would be excited to do on a Sunday afternoon. But working, cleaning and repairing the engine together really strengthened our bonds – and, in the end, they did a fantastic job."

The joys of fatherhood!

Such adventures were put on pause, as the new father decided to take three months of parental leave. He came to Hamburg just in time for the birth of his daughter, Jonna, and to be there for her and his girlfriend, Stella. "Jonna's birth is the most beautiful thing I've ever experienced – simply an incredible feeling!" Jürgens says with delight. "And I have a good feeling about my employer. Seafaring might not always be family-friendly, but Hapag-Lloyd definitely is!"

Was macht Immanuel Jürgens heute?

Im Juli feierte er seinen 37. Geburtstag an Bord der „Hong Kong Express" vor Busan, Südkorea, seiner zweiten Reise nach der Elternzeit. Im September ging's mit Kind und Kegel nach Portugal. Immanual Jürgens genießt die Zeit mit seiner Familie. „Aber Weihnachten werde ich dieses Jahr an Bord verbringen."

What's Immanuel Jürgens doing today?

In July, he celebrated his 37th birthday on board the "Hong Kong Express" off Busan, South Korea, while on his second voyage after parental leave. In September, he and the whole family went to Portugal. He says he will enjoy spending some time with them, adding: "But I'll be spending Christmas on board this year."

Von der Liebe zur Seefahrt und zum Jazz

André Czarnotta

For the love of seafaring and jazz

Kapitän André Czarnotta mag die Weite des Ozeans, Jazz in fast allen Variationen und die Teamarbeit an Bord. Auch wenn er vor zwei Jahren ausstieg, erinnert er sich sehr gern an die vielen Jahre bei Hapag-Lloyd. Das Gespräch fand 2020 vor der sich zuspitzenden Coronavirus-Krise am Hamburger Burchardkai statt. Während an Land die ersten Ausgangsbeschränkungen verhängt werden, sind Kapitän und Crew längst auf dem Atlantik Richtung Cartagena unterwegs und bekommen wenig von den Auswirkungen der weltweiten Pandemie mit, alle Crewmitglieder erfreuen sich bester Gesundheit.

Captain André Czarnotta likes the vastness of the ocean, almost all kinds of jazz, and the camaraderie on board the "Santos Express". Though he quit two years ago, he still has fond memories of his many years with Hapag-Lloyd. Our conversation was held at Hamburg's Container Terminal Burchardkai in 2020 before the coronavirus crisis had started to escalate. By the time the first restrictions on going outside were imposed on land, it had already been some time since the captain and his crew had set sail on the Atlantic Ocean headed for the Colombian port of Cartagena. They felt few of the impacts of the global pandemic, and all crew members are in excellent health.

Vermutlich das einzige Schiff mit Klavier und Congas an Bord: die „Santos Express“ am Hamburger Burchardkai

Probably the only ship with a piano and congas on board: the “Santos Express” at Hamburg’s Container Terminal Burchardkai

<<

Kapitän André Czarnotta sitzt in der Offiziersmesse am Klavier und improvisiert „Maiden Voyage“, eine der berühmtesten Kompositionen des Jazzpianisten Herbie Hancock. „Ich hatte Nachtschicht, muss mich erst ein bisschen einspielen“, entschuldigt er sich. Aber was er da spielt auf der „Santos Express“ am Hamburger Burchardkai, klingt so schön, dass alle Umstehenden innehalten und lauschen. Maiden Voyage, zu Deutsch Jungfernfahrt, passt: Das Klavier hat der Kapitän vor der Übernahme der nagelneuen „Santos Express“ 2017 extra an Bord gebracht. André Czarnotta ist stolz darauf, dass er das Containerschiff in Südkorea abholen durfte. Er steuerte es nach Santos, in den größten Hafen Brasiliens zur Taufe: „Ein unglaubliches Gefühl – eine Ehre!“, schwärmt er.

Die Begeisterung für die Schifffahrt liegt zwar nicht in der Familie, wohl aber an dem Fluss, an dem André Czarnotta aufwuchs: Als Kind stromerte der

Captain André Czarnotta spontaneously sits down at a piano in the officers’ mess and improvises “Maiden Voyage”, one of the most famous compositions of the jazz pianist Herbie Hancock. “I worked the night shift, so I first need to warm up a bit,” he says apologetically. But what he plays on the “Santos Express” at the terminal sounds so beautiful that everyone nearby stops to listen. The song is a fitting one, as the captain had expressly had the piano installed on the “Santos Express” when he took command of the brand-new vessel in 2017. Indeed, Czarnotta is proud to this day that he was permitted to pick up the container ship in South Korea. From there, he brought the vessel to Santos, the largest port in Brazil, for its naming ceremony. “It was an incredible feeling, an honour,” he says with emotion.

Hamburger an der Elbe entlang, träumte sich hinaus in die weite Welt. „Ich bin am Wasser groß geworden, segelte als Jugendlicher mit den Wanderkuttern unseres Segelvereins über die Elbe. Eines Tages mit dem Containerschiff von Hamburg in die Welt zu fahren, das war mein Traum“, so André Czarnotta.

19-jährig bewarb er sich für die Ausbildung zum Schiffsmechaniker bei Hapag-Lloyd und durchlief alle Stationen, Studium inklusive, besitzt sowohl das technische als auch das nautisches Patent. Als junger Mann fuhr er u. a. auf der alten „Leverkusen Express“, drei Jahre auf Pazifik-Atlantik-Express-Diensten und mehrere Jahre auf der „Tsing Tao Express“. „Asien, Mittelmeer, USA, da war alles dabei“, fasst er zusammen.

Gute Lehrer, entspannen mit Yoga, unzählige Kühlcontainer

„Der Wechsel vom Ersten Offizier zum Kapitän ist der größte Schritt“, berichtet André Czarnotta über die Herausforderungen als Führungskraft: „Das Stresslevel ist deutlich höher, weil du jederzeit wissen musst, was zu tun ist. Ich hatte sowohl an der Maschine als auch an Deck sehr gute Lehrer. Das hat mir Kraft gegeben, an mich zu glauben.“ Zum Ausgleich praktiziert Czarnotta regelmäßig Yoga. Führung versteht der Kapitän vor allem als Gemeinschaftsleistung. Nicht jeder müsse alles können, entscheidend sei das richtige Zusammenspiel: „Natürlich gibt es an Bord eine Hierarchie, aber ich versuche meine Mannschaft so wenig zu reglementieren wie möglich. Menschen arbeiten am besten, wenn man ihnen Freiräume ermöglicht.“ Vertrauen und Ehrlichkeit hält er für unerlässlich: „Ein positive Stimmung, ein gutes Gruppengefühl – wenn es drauf ankommt, braucht man genau das!“ So organisiert er mit der Crew gemeinsame Landgänge und Feiern. „Klar

Although a passion for navigation doesn’t run in his family, it is present along the river where Czarnotta grew up. As a child, the Hamburg native would stroll along the Elbe, dreaming of going out into the wider world himself. “I grew up on the water. As a teenager, I sailed on the Elbe in the small cutters of our sailing club. And my dream was to one day be able to sail out into the world from Hamburg on board a container ship,” Czarnotta says.

People perform at their best when you leave them some wiggle room

At 19, Czarnotta applied for an apprenticeship at Hapag-Lloyd to qualify as a ship mechanic. Then, after going through all the remaining stages, including university studies, he finally earned both his engineering and navigating licenses. The postings he had as a young man included one on the old “Leverkusen Express”, three years in the PAX service, and several years on the “Tsing Tao Express”. “Asia, the Mediterranean, the United States – I’ve been everywhere,” he says.

Good teachers, yoga for relaxation, countless refrigerated containers

“The transition from chief officer to captain is the biggest step,” he says while describing the challenges of being a leader. “The stress level is a lot higher because you have to know at all times what needs to be done. But I had very good teachers, both on deck and in the engine room. This has given me strength to believe in myself.” To find some balance, Czarnotta regularly practices yoga.

The captain mainly views leadership as a team effort. Not everyone has to be able to do everything; the crucial factor

müssen in den Häfen der Westküste auch unzählige Kühlcontainer geladen werden. Aber ein Ausflug in Lima, zum Beispiel ins Goldmuseum, ist unvergesslich." Dass die Crew abends nach dem Essen gern zusammensitzt, über Gott und die Welt redet oder ein Kicker-Turnier austrägt, ist für den Kapitän keine Selbstverständlichkeit: „Ich bin dankbar, dass wir uns alle so gut verstehen."

Und wie verträgt sich der Beruf mit dem Familienleben? Kommen seine Söhne Piet und Leo mit der Abwesenheit des Vaters zurecht? „Meine Frau ist super erfinderisch, wenn es darum geht, mich als Papa einzubinden. Als mein erster Sohn noch klein war, hat sie ein Foto von mir übers Bett gehängt und jeden Abend davor gute Nacht gesagt. Als ich nach Monaten nach Hause kam, erkannte mich mein eineinhalbjähriger Sohn sofort, zeigte mit dem Finger auf mich und rief ‚Papa'. Da ging mir das Herz auf." Und noch etwas lieben die Jungs, wenn Papa nach Hause kommt: „Ich habe immer jede Menge Geschenke dabei!", lacht der Kapitän.

——— Die schönste Route und was Jazz und Seefahrt gemeinsam haben

Ein Vorteil der Schifffahrt ist auch, dass der musikbegeisterte Kapitän Original-Instrumente vor Ort kaufen kann. So besitzt er drei Candombé-Congas aus Uruguay, auf denen er Rhythmen von Salsa bis Samba trommelt. Passend zur Lateinamerika-Route der „Santos Express": „Auf dieser Route erlebst du alles, was die Seefahrt so schön macht: erst die europäischen Häfen Hamburg, Rotterdam, Antwerpen, dann die Weite des Atlantiks. Und nachdem du den Panamakanal passiert hast, empfangen dich der Pazifik und die Westküste von Lateinamerika. Hier kann man auch

Beim Tischfußball ist der Rang egal, jeder will gewinnen – und das gelingt im Team am besten, findet André Czarnotta

Czarnotta says that rank doesn't matter at the foosball table. Everyone wants to win – and teamwork is the best path to victorynatoque penatibus.

<<

is the right coordination. "Of course, there is a hierarchy on board, but I try to regiment my crew as little as possible. People perform at their best when you leave them some wiggle room." The level-headed captain considers trust and honesty essential. "A positive spirit, a good sense of camaraderie – when it comes down to it, that's exactly what you need," Czarnotta says. To foster them, he organises shore leaves and parties with his crew. "Countless refrigerated containers obviously have to be loaded in the ports on the west coast, too. But an excursion in Lima, such as to the Gold Museum, is unforgettable." It doesn't always happen that a captain has a crew that likes to sit down and enjoy dinner together, speaks about God and the world, or holds a foosball tournament. "I'm grateful that we all get along so well."

Back home, Czarnotta has a wife and two sons, Piet and Leo. When asked how he reconciles his job with his family life and how they cope with his long absences, he says: "My wife is super resourceful when it comes to getting me involved as Daddy. When my first son was still very small, she hung a photo of me over the bed and said 'good night' to it every night before leaving him alone. And when I came home after months at sea, my one-and-a-half-year-old son recognised me immediately, pointed his finger at me, and said 'Daddy'. I found that really touching." And there's something else that the boys love when Daddy comes home. "I always bring lots of presents!" the captain says with a laugh.

——— The most beautiful route and what jazz and seafaring have in common

Another advantage of being in the shipping business is that the captain can buy original instruments right where they are

noch kleinere Häfen und das ursprüngliche Land hautnah erleben. Diese Route ist die wohl schönste, die ich je gefahren bin."

Menschen arbeiten am besten, wenn man ihnen Freiräume ermöglicht

Wann immer möglich, nutzt André Czarnotta die knappe Freizeit an Bord und setzt sich ans Klavier. Dann klappt er das Real Book, die Noten-Bibel aller Jazzer, auf und taucht ein in die Welt der Improvisation. „Es ist ein bisschen wie bei der Seefahrt, sobald du die Grundregeln beherrscht, kannst du dich frei bewegen. Und das ist Jazz für mich: unglaubliche Freiheit." Hat er einen Tipp, wie Menschen Zugang zur Jazzmusik finden, die normalerweise wenig damit anfangen können? „John Coltrane kann ich nur jedem empfehlen! Wie er den Song ‚My Favorite Things' mit seinem Quartett interpretiert, das ist fantastisch." Seine „Favorite Things" hat Kapitän André Czarnotta längst gefunden.

made. For example, he owns three Candombé congas from Uruguay, on which he drums rhythms from salsa to samba. Given these interests, the Latin America route of the "Santos Express" is a good fit for Czarnotta. "On this route, you get to experience everything that makes seafaring so beautiful: first the European ports of Hamburg, Rotterdam and Antwerp, and then the vastness of the Atlantic," he says. "And after you've passed through the Panama Canal, you are welcomed by the Pacific and the west coast of Latin America. There, you can also enjoy even smaller ports and look out on untouched countryside from up close. This route is probably the most beautiful one I've ever sailed on."

Whenever possible, Czarnotta uses the little free time he has on board to sit down at the piano. Then he opens up the Real Book, the music bible of all jazz musicians, and immerses himself in the world of improvisation. "It's a bit like seafaring: Once you've mastered the rules, you can move about freely. And that's jazz for me: incredible freedom." When asked if he has a tip for how to make jazz a bit more accessible to people who don't know much about it, he says: "I can only recommend John Coltrane to everyone! The way he interprets the song 'My Favorite Things' with his quartet is fantastic." For his part, Captain Czarnotta found his favourite things a long time ago.

Was macht André Czarnotta heute?

Der erfahrene Kapitän hat Hapag-Lloyd mittlerweile verlassen, weil er mehr Zeit mit seiner Familie verbringen will. „Nach so vielen Jahren Seefahrt ist es auch mal gut gewesen", findet André Czarnotta. Seine einjährige Auszeit nutzte der begeisterte Musiker, um Klavier, Gitarre und Congas zu spielen. Und auch, um neue Bandprojekte anzuschieben. Und jobmäßig? „Aktuell bringe ich mit einem Highspeedkatamaran Techniker zu ihren Windmühlen in einem Windpark in der Nordsee. Mal sehen, was die Zukunft bringt …"

What's André Czarnotta doing today?

The seasoned captain has since left Hapag-Lloyd because he wants to spend more time with his family. "After so many years at sea, it's time for a change," Czarnotta says. The avid musician used his one-year sabbatical to play the piano, guitar and congas – and to try to get some new band projects going. But what about work? "I am currently taking technicians to their turbines in a North Sea wind farm on a high-speed catamaran. We'll see what the future holds…"

Vom Matrosen zum Personalchef

Christian Müller

From ordinary seaman to head of HR

Als Matrose fuhr Christian Müller Ende der 1950er-Jahre nach Süd- und Nordamerika, erlebte die Entstehung der Containerschifffahrt und die Fusion von Hapag-Lloyd hautnah. In London und San Francisco arbeitete er als Operator, bevor er die Kreuzschifffahrt für sich entdeckte – und schließlich Personalchef wurde. Hier erzählt der Kapitän a. D. von seinen Anfängen, welche Chancen sich in den 1970er-Jahren für Nautiker ergaben und warum er stolz ist, dass bis heute in der Personalabteilung erfahrene Seeleute das Sagen haben.

As an ordinary seaman, Christian Müller sailed to South and North America in the 1950s, witnessed the emergence of container shipping, and experienced the merger that created Hapag-Lloyd at first hand. He worked as an operator in London and San Francisco before discovering a passion for cruise shipping – and eventually becoming a personnel manager. Here, the retired captain talks about his beginnings, the opportunities that arose for navigators in the 1970s, and why he is proud that experienced seafarers still call the shots in the HR Department today.

Zuhause am Wasser: Nach vielen Jahren im Ausland lebt Christian Müller wieder in seiner Heimat Bremen in der Nähe des Werdersees

At home on the water: After many years abroad, Müller lives again near the Werdersee lake in his hometown of Bremen

<<

Habenhausen ist ein idyllischer, fast ländlicher Stadtteil der Hansestadt Bremen. Nördlich begrenzt vom Werdersee, östlich fließt die Weser vorbei. Gemütliche Einfamilienhäuser säumen die ruhigen Straßen, das Naherholungsgebiet gleich um die Ecke lädt zu langen Spaziergängen ein. Von hier spazierte der 17-jährige Christian Müller 1957 in die weite Welt. „Mein Vater arbeitete nach dem Zweiten Weltkrieg als Hausarzt, er war weit und breit der Einzige mit einer riesigen Praxis und hatte mich als Nachfolger im Sinn. Aber das altsprachliche Gymnasium, auf das er mich schickte, war nichts für mich, ich bin gescheitert – zum Glück! Auf der nächsten Schule lernte ich im April 1956 meine zukünftige Frau kennen.“ Die Augen des heute 82-jährigen leuchten, Gattin Marianne sitzt an seiner Seite am gedeckten Gartentisch und verdreht spöttisch liebevoll die Augen: „Du sollst doch von der Seefahrt erzählen!“ Ohne seine

Habenhausen is an idyllic, almost rural district of the Hanseatic city of Bremen. The Werdersee lake lies to its north, and the Weser River flows along its eastern side. Its quiet streets are lined with cosy, single-family homes, and the recreational area just around the corner is a perfect place to take long walks.

In 1957, a then-17-year-old Christian Müller ventured out from here into the wider world. “My father worked as a general practitioner after the Second World War,” Müller recounts. “He was the only one around for miles, ran a huge practice, and had me in mind as his successor. But the high school he sent me to, where we learned ancient languages, wasn’t for me – and I luckily failed out! I met my future wife at the next school in April 1956.”

The eyes of the now 81-year-old shine. Sitting at his side at the well-laid

Frau wären die Anfänge der Fahrten aber nur halb so romantisch gewesen, findet Christian Müller: „Marianne ging 1960 für ein Jahr als Au-Pair nach Amerika. Da war ich gerade Matrose beim Norddeutschen Lloyd geworden. Ich setzte mich aufs Rad, fuhr zur Heuerstelle in den Überseehafen und fragte, ob ich ein Schiff zur Westküste Nord bekommen könnte." Wenige Wochen später wartete Marianne „zufällig" am Pier von Long Beach auf ihn. Mutter und Großmutter hatten die Begegnung eingefädelt. Aus dem lockeren Liebelei wurde eine feste Beziehung und obwohl es der Kapitän der „Bartenstein" kritisch beäugte, stieg Marianne auf der Rückreise an Bord und fuhr gemeinsam mit ihrem Zukünftigen zurück in die Heimat. Selbstverständlich in getrennten Kabinen.

______ Post aus Chile, Fahrten mit Kaffee und Baumwolle, Erster Offizier nach der Fusion

Gut sechzig Jahre später erinnert sich Christian Müller daran wie gestern und ebenso an die vielen Stationen seiner Tätigkeit für Hapag-Lloyd. Gerade kürzlich steckte der Kapitän seine markante Nase wieder mal in die Vergangenheit: Unzähligen Briefe und Tonbänder, die sowohl er als auch die drei Söhne und seine Frau über die Jahre hin- und herschickten, lagern im Keller. „Ich fand einen Brief aus Chile, in dem ich den Kindern den Besuch einer katholischen Kirche in Antofagasta ausführlich beschrieb – aber katholisch war ich nie", lacht der Kapitän. Die ersten Jahre, als die Jungs klein waren, seien hart gewesen, berichtet der Bremer und seine Frau nickt: „Wenn Christian losfuhr, habe ich erst mal das ganze Haus von oben bis unten geputzt – dann trat eine große Leere ein. Obwohl ich mit den Jungs genug zu tun hatte, vermisste ich meinen Mann sehr."

garden table is his wife, Marianne, who mockingly but affectionately rolls her eyes before saying: "Come on! You're supposed to talk about seafaring!" But Müller thinks that the beginnings of his voyages would have only been half as romantic without his wife.

From Miami to Manila – as an operator you can work all over the world

"In 1960, Marianne went to the United States for a year to work as an au pair," he says. "I had just started working as an ordinary seaman for North German Lloyd. I got on my bike, rode to the seamen's employment office in the overseas harbour, and asked if I could get a ship to the northern part of the West Coast of the Americas." A few weeks later, Marianne "happened" to be waiting for him at the pier in Long Beach. Mother and grandmother had arranged the encounter. The casual flirtation turned into a steady relationship. And even though the captain of the "Bartenstein" frowned upon it, Marianne boarded the ship for its return voyage and sailed back home together with her future husband – in separate cabins, of course.

______ Mail from Chile, voyages with coffee and cotton, chief mate after the merger

Over 60 years later, Müller still remembers all this – and the many stages of his career with Hapag-Lloyd – as if it were yesterday. Just recently, the captain stuck his prominent nose into the past once again. Countless letters and audiotapes that he, his wife and his three sons mailed each other over the years are stored in the cellar. "I found a letter from Chile in which I described in detail to the children

„Liebenstein“, „Buntenstein“, „Moselstein“ hießen u. a. die Schiffe, mit denen Christian Müller als Vierter, Dritter und Zweiter Offizier unterwegs war. „Die meisten Fahrten gingen nach Mittelamerika, wir luden Kaffee und Baumwolle, krochen noch selbst durch die Laderäume, das war schwere körperliche Arbeit“, erinnert er sich. Mit der Fusion des Norddeutschen Lloyd mit der HAPAG 1970 und der einsetzenden Containerschifffahrt änderte sich dann nicht nur die Arbeitsweise und die Einsatzgebiete – Christian Müller wurde auch als Erster des Norddeutschen Lloyd zum Ersten Offizier befördert: „Ich kehrte gerade von einer dreimonatigen Reise zurück, als der Anruf kam, ob ich am nächsten Tag einspringen könne Richtung Brasilien – meine Frau war nicht gerade begeistert, es gab Tränen. Aber nachdem wir ausgehandelt hatten, dass sie auf der nächsten Reise mitfahren durfte, sagte ich zu.“

Von Miami bis Manila: Als Operator kannst du auf der ganzen Welt arbeiten

Als Operator nach London und San Francisco

Die Fusion der Hamburger mit der Bremer Reederei zu Hapag-Lloyd brachte Veränderungen für viele Seeleute – Christian Müller berichtet von den Chancen, die sich dadurch für Nautiker ergaben: „Auch wenn auf dem Wasser durch die neuen Containerschiffe weniger Personal gebraucht wurde: Der Bedarf an Land wuchs weltweit. Miami, Hongkong, Singapur, Manila – du konntest als Operator in der ganzen Welt arbeiten.“ So sehr er seine Jahre auf See, die langen Liegezeiten in Sydney inklusive Opernbesuch oder die Ausflüge mit weißem Chevrolet in San

my visit to a Catholic church in Antofagasta – but I was never Catholic,” the captain notes with a laugh.

He says that the first years, when the boys were small, were hard. Nodding, his wife adds: “Whenever Christian set sail, I would first clean the entire house from top to bottom. But then a profound emptiness would set in. Although I had plenty to do with the boys, I missed my husband a lot.”

Müller sailed on many different vessels – including the “Liebenstein”, the “Buntenstein” and the “Moselstein” – as a fourth, third and second officer. “Most of my voyages were to Central America,” he recalls. “We loaded coffee and cotton, still crawling through the holds ourselves. That was tough physical labour.”

The emergence of container shipping and Hapag’s merger with North German Lloyd in 1970 led to changes in working methods and areas of operation. What’s more, Müller was the first former employee of North German Lloyd to be promoted to chief mate. “I had just returned from a three-month voyage when the call came asking if I could fill in on a ship departing for Brazil the next day,” he recounts. “My wife wasn’t exactly thrilled, and there were some tears. But after we negotiated that she could come along on the next voyage, I accepted the offer.”

Working as an operator in London and San Francisco

The merger of the Hamburg- and Bremen-based shipping lines to form Hapag-Lloyd resulted in changes for many seafarers – but it also created a lot of fresh opportunities for navigators.
“The new container ships meant that fewer staff were needed at sea,” Müller explains. “But the demand for shore-based

Von der Weser in die weite Welt: Christian Müller arbeitete zu Wasser und zu Lande für Hapag-Lloyd – sogar mal auf einem Kreuzfahrtschiff

From the Weser into the wide world: Müller worked for Hapag-Lloyd at sea and on shore – including once on a cruise ship

>>

Zwei mit Geschichte: vorn Christian Müller, hinten rechts der berühmte Dreimaster „Alexander von Humboldt"

Two with long histories: Müller with the famous three-master the "Alexander von Humboldt" behind him to the right

Francisco genossen hatte: „Als ich 1979 gefragt wurde für drei Jahre nach London zu gehen, um dort die Befrachtung unserer Schiffe zu organisieren, musste ich nicht lange überlegen – mit Sack und Pack zogen wir an die Themse!" Die Arbeit im Konsortium mit Kollegen anderer Reedereien war neu und interessant, das Leben in der britischen Metropole familienfreundlich. „Unsere Kinder konnten mit dem Rad zur Deutschen Schule und zum Tennis fahren, meine Frau sprach ohnehin gut Englisch, verbesserte ihre Kenntnisse noch auf der Abendschule

employees grew worldwide. Miami, Hong Kong, Singapore, Manila – you could work as an operator all over the world."

Of course, he loved his years at sea, which included long layovers in Sydney with visits to the opera house and excursions in a white Chevrolet in San Francisco. But that didn't keep him from embracing new challenges and opportunities. "In 1979, when I was asked to go to London for three years to organise the chartering of our ships, I didn't have to think twice," he says. "We packed all our belongings and moved to the Thames!"

und studierte Kunstgeschichte“, erinnert sich Christian Müller. Nach drei Jahren schickte ihn Hapag-Lloyd 1983 wieder auf große Fahrt. „Aber schon auf der zweiten Reise mit der ‚Sierra Express‘ Richtung Südamerika erhielt ich einen Anruf – es war eines der ersten Schiffe mit Telefon – ob ich mir vorstellen könne, nach San Francisco zu gehen, es gäbe einen Deal mit der amerikanischen Schifffahrtsgesellschaft ‚SeaLand‘. So zogen wir mit unserem Jüngsten 1985 für ein Jahr an die Westküste.“ Kaum zurück in Bremen, Kapitän Müller wollte gerade die Wohnzimmerwände streichen, die Umzugscontainer war noch unterwegs, meldete sich die Personalabteilung – und hatte erneut London im Angebot: „Innerhalb von 24 Stunden mussten wir uns entscheiden und zogen 1986 kurzerhand ein weiteres Mal um. Die internationale Arbeit mit den Kollegen war abwechslungsreich und gefiel mir persönlich mindestens so gut wie die Seefahrt.“

______ Rauf aufs Kreuzfahrtschiff und endlich Kapitän

„Müller, wir wollen Sie auf der ‚Europa‘ haben!“, sagte der Personalchef eines Tages am Telefon. Christian Müller lacht: „Ich reagierte verdutzt, bisher fuhren da doch immer Kollegen, die mindestens ein ‚von‘ im Nachnamen hatten.“ Aber mit der Aussicht als Kapitän über die Meere zu fahren, war die „Europa“ ein gute Option. „Erst mal wurde ich auf der ‚Leverkusen Express‘ in Vancouver 1989 zum Kapitän ernannt“, erzählt Christian Müller stolz: „Ich fuhr als Erster Offizier hin, dann drückte mir der Kapitän mein Beförderungsschreiben in die Hand. Draußen wartete schon sein Wohnmobil, mit dem er eine Tour nach Alaska startete.“ Staff-Kapitän auf der „Europa“ war eine weitere neue Herausforderung. „So gut ich mich in der Befrachtung unserer Schiffe

Working in the consortium with colleagues from other shipping companies was new and interesting, and life in the British metropolis was family-friendly. “Our children could cycle to the German school and to tennis. And my wife, who already spoke good English anyways, got even better at it with evening classes, and then studied art history at a university,” Müller recalls.

Visits to the opera house in Sydney, excursions in a white Chevrolet in San Francisco

After three years, in 1983, Hapag-Lloyd assigned him to work at sea again. “But already on the second voyage with the ‘Sierra Express’ heading to South America, I received a call,” he says, noting that it was one of the first ships with a telephone. “They wanted to know if I could imagine going to San Francisco, as there was supposed to be a deal with the American shipping company SeaLand. So, in 1985, we moved with our youngest son to the West Coast for a year.”

Right after returning to Bremen, Müller was about to start painting the living room walls. But then he received a call from the HR Department, which was offering him a chance to move back to London. “We had 24 hours to make up our minds,” he says. “So we moved again in 1986.”

______ Shifting to cruise ships – and a captain at last

“Then, one day, the personnel manager called and said: ‘Müller, we want you on the ‘Europa’!” Müller recounts with a laugh. “I was puzzled, as my colleagues who had sailed on that cruise ship so far had always had at least one ‘von’ in their

und der Navigation auskannte, jetzt war ich für sämtliche Belange der Besatzung verantwortlich. Ob Streitereien unter Seemännern, die geräuschlos geschlichtet werden mussten, Verhandlungen mit dem Betriebsrat oder neue Matratzen für die Besatzung, all das landete bei mir.“

Ich wollte gerade ein Fahrrad kaufen, als mich der Notruf eines Offiziers erreichte

Abwechslungsreiche Jahre in der Konzernzentrale und die Sache mit dem Rücken

Insgesamt drei Jahre fuhr Christian Müller auf der „Europa“, wechselte zwischendurch wieder in die Containerschifffahrt, bis sich ein neuer Job an Land ergab: Die Leitung der Personalabteilung von Hapag-Lloyd am Ballindamm. Und hier konnte er die Summe all seiner Erfahrungen einbringen. Christian Müller begleitete das Projekt „Schiff der Zukunft“, organisierte das Recruiting der Philippinischen Seeleute Mitte der 1990er, kümmerte sich gemeinsam mit seinem Team um Weiterbildung und Kurse für die Kollegen, die nach der Wende neuen Jobs bei Hapag-Lloyd fanden. „Acht Jahre, in denen ich die Seefahrt noch mal aus einer völlig neuen Perspektive kennenlernte.“ Und er setzte alle Hebel in Bewegung, wenn irgendwo auf hoher See Unvorhergesehenes eintrat: „Ich war gerade in Bremen unterwegs, ein Fahrrad kaufen, als mich der Notruf eines Ersten Offiziers erreichte. Bei schlechtem Wetter hatte sich der Kapitän schwer verletzt – er war bei einem Rundgang bei hoher Dünung gegen die Ankerwinde geschleudert worden. Ich sagte nur ‚Sie müssen darauf bestehen, dass ein Hubschrauber kommt, sonst stirbt der Kapitän!‘, der Hubschrauber

last name,” he adds, indicating that they came from families with ties to Germany’s nobility. But with the prospect of sailing the seas as a captain, the “Europa” was a good option. “I was first named captain on the ‘Leverkusen Express’ in Vancouver in 1989,” Müller proudly recalls. “I sailed there as chief officer, and then the captain pressed my promotion letter into my hand. His camper van was already waiting for him outside, and then he started off on a trip to Alaska.” Being the staff captain – or second in command – on the “Europa” was another new challenge. “I was already very familiar with the chartering of our ships and navigation, but now I was also responsible for all matters related to the crew,” he says. “Whether it was disputes among seafarers that had to be settled quietly, negotiations with the works council, or getting new mattresses for the crew – all of that ended up being my job to handle.”

Eventful years at the corporate headquarters and some stubborn back issues

Müller sailed on the “Europa” for a total of three years, though he switched back to container shipping a few times during this period. But then a new shore-based job popped up: to be head of Hapag-Lloyd’s Maritime HR Department, based at the company’s headquarters on the Ballindamm in Hamburg.

This was the job in which he was able to bring together his very broad range of experiences. Müller assisted with the “Ship of the Future” project, organised the recruiting of Filipino seafarers in the mid-1990s, and – together with his team – arranged additional training and courses for the colleagues who found new jobs with Hapag-Lloyd after Germany’s reunification. He describes this time as “eight years in which I got to know seafaring again from a completely new perspective”.

holte den Verletzten ab, allerdings bekam ich keinen Kontakt zu dem Krankenhaus irgendwo in Süd-Irland." Kurzerhand rief Christian Müller seinen Sohn an, der mittlerweile als Arzt in Mainz arbeitete, und bat ihn um Unterstützung. „Er fand über seine Kanäle heraus, dass der Oberarzt der Klinik beim Fischen war – und sorgte dafür, dass dieser sofort zurückkehrte. Der Kapitän wurde dann in die nächstgrößere Klinik nach Cork geflogen. Später ließen wir ihn nach Bremen verlegen, wo ich ihn dann besuchte."

In den letzten Jahren hatte der Personalchef selbst mit Schmerzen zu kämpfen: „Mein Rücken spielte nicht mehr mit. 2001, nach vielen wunderbaren Jahren bei Hapag-Lloyd reichte ich die Kündigung ein." Mittlerweile geht es dem sportlichen 82-Jährigen gut, „Ich kann sogar wieder Tennis spielen", freut sich der Kapitän und Personalchef a. D. Immer noch interessiert ihn, was bei Hapag-Lloyd passiert, so auch den Einstieg beim JadeWeserPort Wilhelmshaven: „Es gibt viele Gründe, diesen Weg einzuschlagen: größere Containerschiffe in Bezug auf Länge, Breite und Tiefgang, kurze Revierfahrten im Vergleich zu Hamburg und Bremerhaven und Konkurrenzfähigkeit zu Rotterdam und Antwerpen." Dass in der Personalabteilung erfahrene Seeleute das Sagen haben, findet Christian Müller unverzichtbar: „Das gehört zu den großen Stärken von Hapag-Lloyd!"

And he made every effort whenever something unforeseen happened somewhere on the high seas. "I was on my way to Bremen to buy a bicycle when I received a distress call from a chief mate," he recalls. "In rough weather, the captain had been seriously injured. I only said, 'You must insist that a helicopter comes, or the captain will die!' A helicopter eventually did pick up the casualty, but I wasn't able to get in touch with the hospital somewhere in southern Ireland." Müller called one of his sons, who was now working as a doctor in Mainz, and asked him for help. "He was able to figure out that the senior physician at the clinic was out fishing – and he made sure that he returned immediately," Müller says. "The captain was then flown to the nearest hospital, in Cork. Later, we had him transferred to Bremen, where I went to visit him."

In his last few years on the job, the head of HR struggled with his own pains. "My back was no longer cooperating. So, in 2001, after many wonderful years with Hapag-Lloyd, I handed in my resignation."

Today, the sporty 82-year-old is doing well and happily says he "can even play tennis again". He still keeps close track of current events, including Hapag-Lloyd's recent investment in JadeWeserPort Wilhelmshaven. "There are a lot of good reasons to follow this path: larger container ships, short pilotage waters compared to Hamburg and Bremerhaven, and competitiveness with Rotterdam and Antwerp." Müller also finds it necessary to have experienced seafarers still call the shots in the HR Department. "That is one of the great strengths of Hapag-Lloyd!"

Was macht Christian Müller heute?

Er meldet sich ganz modern per WhatsApp: „Wir sind hier rundum zufrieden! Meine Frau Marianne und ich haben durch meinen Beruf viele tolle Menschen kennengelernt und Freunde gefunden. Auch unsere Söhne, ein Journalist und zwei Ärzte, profitierten vom Leben eines Seemanns, der in London und San Francisco tätig war. Mein größtes Glück ist, dass ich seit 59 Jahren eine Frau an meiner Seite habe, die alles mitgemacht hat."

What's Christian Müller doing today?

He answers in a very modern way – via WhatsApp: "We're totally happy here! My wife, Marianne, and I have met a lot of great people and made friends through my job. Our sons – one journalist and two doctors – also benefited from the life of a seafarer who worked in London and San Francisco. My greatest fortune is that I've had a wife who stayed by my side and through it all for 59 years."

Notausgang

Karriereschub mitten in der Pandemie

Sylwester Mackiewicz

Career boost in the middle of the pandemic

Ein sonniger Wintertag in Bremerhaven, majestätisch erhebt sich die „Al Bahia" am Kaiserkai der Bredo Werft an der Weser. Der Lärm von Hämmern und Schleifen ist schon von Weitem zu hören, an Deck fliegen Funken bei Schweißarbeiten. Die Crew erledigt hier ein paar Schönheitsreparaturen auf dem 2008 erbauten Containerriesen, der über eine Kapazität von 7.300 TEU verfügt. Kapitän Sylwester Mackiewicz hat einiges zu tun, nimmt sich aber Zeit für ein Interview.

On a sunny winter day in Bremerhaven, the "Al Bahia" rises up majestically in the Kaiserdock of the Bredo shipyard on the Weser River. The sound of hammers and grinding can be heard from far away, and sparks fly as welding is performed on the deck. The crew has been taking care of some cosmetic repairs on the giant container ship, which was built in 2008 and has a capacity of 7,300 TEU. Captain Sylwester Mackiewicz has a lot to do, but takes time for a talk.

Helm statt Kapitäns-mütze: Sylwester Mackiewicz während der Reparaturarbeiten auf der „Al Bahia" in Bremerhaven

Helmet instead of captain's cap: Mackiewicz during repair work on the "Al Bahia" in Bremerhaven

<<

Es sind schon verrückte Zeiten", erzählt Sylwester Mackiewicz, während er die Kaffeemaschine einschaltet und zwei Teller mit Aufschnitt, dazu Pumpernickel und Frischkäse serviert. Er trägt Jeans und einen dunkelblauen Pullover mit den obligatorischen vier goldenen Streifen rechts und links auf den Schultern. „Ich fahre hauptsächlich die Europa-Asienroute und wir hörten schon Ende 2019, dass da ein neuartiges Virus in China die Runde macht. Aber so richtig ernst nahmen wir das nicht. Wir gingen an Land, ohne zu wissen, wie gefährlich sich die Situation noch entwickeln würde – es war der Anfang der Pandemie."

Der 51-Jährige arbeitete zu dieser Zeit noch als Chief Mate. „Im Februar erlebten wir dann im Hafen von Shanghai hautnah die Auswirkungen. Niemand kam mehr an Bord, alles wurde nur noch per Mail erledigt. Und natürlich gab es keinen Landurlaub. Nur ein Agent und zwei Beamte besuchten uns zur Personenkon-

These are some really crazy times," Sylwester Mackiewicz says while he turns on the coffee machine and sets out two plates full of cold cuts, pumpernickel bread and cream cheese. He is wearing a dark blue sweater with the obligatory four gold stripes on the right and left shoulders. "I mainly sail on the Europe-Asia route, and we already heard in late 2019 that there was a new kind of virus circulating in China. But we didn't really take it that seriously. We went ashore not knowing how dangerous the situation was going to get, as it was only the beginning of the pandemic."

At the time, the 51-year-old was still working as a chief mate. "Then, in February, we saw the impacts up close and personal in the Port of Shanghai. No one came on board anymore, and everything was done via email. And, of course, there

trolle im Konferenzraum, von Kopf bis Fuß in Schutzanzügen, mit Gummihandschuhen und doppelten Gesichtsmasken bekleidet." Die Offiziersassistenten hätten regelrecht Angst vor den fremd anmutenden Kollegen gehabt: „Aber ich sagte nur: ‚Ihr sollte lieber Angst vor Leuten haben, die ohne Schutzkleidung an Bord kommen'", lacht Sylwester Mackiewicz. Fast sechs Monate schipperte der gebürtige Pole zwischen den Lockdowns in China und Europa hin und her. „In China kam der Lockdown nach unserer Abreise. Kaum hatten wir dann Europa wieder verlassen, setzte dort der Lockdown ein. Aber wenn du auf dem Schiff bist und fast alles remote erledigst, lebst du wie auf einer Insel. Wir fühlten uns jederzeit sicher."

Die Frage aller Fragen: „Wollen Sie Kapitän werden?"

Im Mai kam die verdiente Pause und Zeit für Tochter, Sohn und Frau. Zeit, im neuen Haus am Stettiner Stadtrand zu werkeln und ein bisschen Urlaub im nahen Barlinek zu machen. „Dann klingelte das Telefon und Finn Albertsen stellte sich als neuer Director Crew Management & Training für die aus Dubai gemanagte Flotte vor: ‚Könnten Sie in Kürze wieder an Bord gehen – als Kapitän?', fragte er mich und lud mich zum Vorstellungsgespräch ein", erzählt Sylwester Mackiewicz. Wie man sich fühlt, wenn man über 17 Jahre als Chief Mate die Weltmeere bereist hat und dann die Frage aller Fragen gestellt bekommt, kann man sich unschwer vorstellen. „Ehrlicherweise hatte ich in den letzten Jahren schon überlegt, vielleicht noch mal etwas völlig anderes zu machen", gibt der Mann mit den strahlend blauen Augen zu. „Aber das war nach diesem Telefonat vom Tisch. Auch meine Frau sagte: Diese Gelegenheit kriegst du kein zweites Mal!"

So absolvierte der erfahrene Seemann, der in seinen Jahren als Erster

wasn't any shore leave. We were only visited for a personnel identity check by one agent and two officials – dressed from head to t oe in protective suits, rubber gloves and double face masks." The officer cadets, he continues, were really frightened by the strange-looking people. "But I only said: 'You should be more afraid of people who come on board without protective clothing,'" he adds with a laugh.

When you're on a ship doing almost everything remotely, it's like living on an island

For almost six months, the native of Poland sailed back and forth between the lockdowns in China and Europe. "China went into lockdown after we had departed. And right after we left Europe again, the lockdown started there. But when you're on a ship and doing almost everything remotely, it's like you're living on an island. We felt safe at all times."

The question of all questions: "Do you want to be a captain?"

In May, it came time for a well-deserved break and time with his wife, son and daughter. He also had time to work on his new house on the outskirts of Szczecin and to enjoy a brief holiday in the nearby town of Barlinek. "Then the phone rang, and Finn Albertsen introduced himself as the new Director Crew Management & Training for the fleet managed from Dubai. 'Could you come back on board again soon – as a captain?' he asked me and invited me for an interview," Mackiewicz recounts.

It's easy to imagine how one feels after sailing the world's oceans as a chief mate for over 17 years and then being

Offizier die unterschiedlichsten Kapitänscharaktere studieren konnte, an einem Sonntagmorgen online zwei Vorstellungsrunden. „Es ging ums gesamte Know-how an Bord. Schiffsdokumente und Zertifikate, IMS-Verfahren und was in unerwarteten Situationen zu tun ist, zum Beispiel bei Maschinenausfällen, Piraterie oder Unfällen an Bord. Auch wie ich die Besatzung in der aktuellen Pandemie manage, wenn beispielsweise Verträge verlängert werden müssen, weil keine Abreisemöglichkeit besteht." Fragen, die man nicht mit dem Lehrbuch in der Hand, sondern nur mit jahrelanger Erfahrung beantworten kann, glaubt Sylwester Mackiewicz. Es folgte banges Warten und schließlich die ersehnte Zusage „Danach haben meine Frau und ich erst mal einen Champagner aufgemacht!"

Ich überprüfe alles zwei Mal, schließlich bin ich für alles verantwortlich

Verantwortung tragen, die Crew beruhigen, Geschichten und Geschenke aus aller Welt

„Meiner erste Fahrt in neuer Rolle war großartig, denn ich hatte eine sehr gute und lange Übergabezeit", berichtet der frisch beförderte Kapitän augenzwinkernd: „Eigentlich sollte es eine zehntägige Übergabe von Hamburg nach New York werden. Aber kurz vor Ankunft stellte der begleitende Kapitän fest, dass sein Visum abgelaufen war – so durfte er nicht an Land und wir machten die gesamte Tour zusammen." Charleston, Savannah, Le Havre, London, Rotterdam, Hamburg – Häfen, die Sylwester Mackiewicz unzählige Male als Chief Mate angefahren hatte, steuerte er jetzt als Kapitän an. „Und ganz ehrlich: Früher habe ich manchmal

asked the question of all questions. "To be honest, for the last few years, I'd been thinking about maybe doing something completely different," admits this man with bright blue eyes. "But that was out of the question after this phone call. And my wife also said to me: 'You won't get this opportunity a second time.'"
So, on a Sunday morning, the veteran seafarer – who had been able to study the characteristics of a wide range of captains over his years as a chief officer – completed two rounds of online interviews. "It was about everything you had to know on board, such as ship documents and certificates, IMS procedures and what you should do in unexpected situations, such as engine failures, pirate attacks or accidents on board. And it also touched on how I would manage the crew during the ongoing pandemic, such as if contracts have to be extended because it's impossible to disembark." As Mackiewicz sees it, these are questions that can't be answered with a textbook in your hand, but only with years of experience.

Then there was a lot of anxious anticipation before the long-awaited decision finally arrived. "After that, the first thing my wife and I did was pop open a bottle of champagne!" he says.

Taking command, reassuring the crew, stories and gifts from around the world.

"My first voyage in my new role was fantastic because I had a very good and long handover period," the freshly minted captain says with a wink. "I was actually supposed to have a 10-day handover sailing from Hamburg to New York. But shortly before arriving, the captain who was supposed to shadow me discovered that his visa had expired – so he wasn't permitted ashore and we

Oben angekommen: Gleich nach der Beförderung bewies Sylwester Mackiewicz, dass er auch heikle Situationen im Griff hat

Arrived at the top: Right after being promoted, Mackiewicz proved that he can also handle tricky situations

>>

Der Nordsee so nah: Der Blick von der Brücke über den Hafen reicht bis zur Helgoländer Bucht

Close to the North Sea: the view from the bridge over the harbour reaches as far as Helgoland Bay

gedacht, na ja, so viel macht ein Kapitän nun auch nicht. Aber jetzt weiß ich, was Verantwortung bedeutet. Gerade in diesen Zeiten, wenn du noch viel intensiver für deine Crew da sein musst, und durch Covid 19 weltweit so viel Unsicherheit herrscht."

Aktuell sei er weit davon entfernt einen Routine-Job zu machen. „Ich überprüfe alles zwei Mal, lerne viel Neues, schließlich bin ich für alles, was ich tue, verantwortlich." Auch in Sachen Personalverantwortung und Kommunikation kann er jetzt seine Erfahrung einbringen.

did the whole tour together." Charleston, Savannah, Le Havre, London, Rotterdam, Hamburg – ports that Mackiewicz had called at countless times as a chief mate he was now sailing into as a captain. "And, to be completely honest, I sometimes used to think 'Oh well, a captain doesn't really do that much.' But now I know what responsibility means – especially in these times when you have to be there so much more for your crew and there's so much uncertainty across the world due to Covid-19."

At the moment, he continues, his job is still far from having become routine.

„Einmal mehr wird mir klar, wie viel Wahrheit in einem Satz aus dem Vorstellungsgespräch liegt: „Ein Kapitän ist nur so gut wie seine Besatzung." Der schwere Unfall eines Bootsmannes an Bord brachte ihn an seine Grenzen, aber am Ende meisterte er die Situation und konnte seine Crew beruhigen. Es sei hart gewesen, aber man habe es gemeinsam durchgestanden. „Hapag-Lloyd pflegt eine No-Blame-Kultur, das schätze ich sehr, denn wir sind alle fehlbar." Wie sehr er selbst als junger Mann von Wertschätzung und Vertrauen seiner Vorgesetzten profitierte, hat er auch nach vielen Jahren nicht vergessen: „Als ich 1994 als Kadett auf meine erste Fahrt nach Südamerika ging, waren viele alte Seebären mit an Bord. Wir haben hart geschuftet, aber die Alten haben uns Junge gut behandelt und in den Häfen immer die Zeche bezahlt – denn viel verdient haben wir nicht", erinnert er sich und schwärmt von alten Zeiten: „Mit Kühlschiffen Bananen aus Ecuador, Kolumbien und der Karibik zu holen. Ananas aus Südafrika, Kiwis aus Neuseeland und Australien – das war toll! Und überall bekamen wir riesige Paletten Obst geschenkt."

______ Weniger Papierkram, mehr Weihnachten mit „Kevin – allein zu Haus"

Unvergessen der Karneval und die Fußballweltmeisterschaft in Rio: „Die Liegezeiten waren lang, da konnten wir richtig mitfeiern, man ging ohne große Kontrollen von Bord und kam irgendwann zurück." In dieser Zeit habe er erlebt, wofür er als Junge seinen zehn Jahre älteren Bruder bewundert und beneidet habe: „Wir lebten in Polen hinter dem Eisernen Vorhang, aber er durfte raus und brachte Geschichten und Geschenke aus aller Welt mit."

Was die Zukunft bringt und wie sich die Schifffahrt durch die Pandemie

"I'm checking everything twice and learning a lot of new things – after all, I'm responsible for everything I do". His experience also helps him now when it comes to communication and his responsibility for the crew. "Once again, I realize just how much truth there is in something I heard in one of my interviews: 'A captain is only as good as his crew.'" A serious accident involving a bosun pushed him to his limits, but he was ultimately able to gain control of the situation and reassure his crew. It was hard, he says, but they got through it together. "Hapag-Lloyd fosters a no-blame culture, which I appreciate very much because we can all make mistakes."

Hapag-Lloyd fosters a no-blame culture, which I appreciate very much

After many years, he still hasn't forgotten how much he benefited himself from the appreciation and trust of his superiors as a young man. "When I went on my first voyage as a cadet to South America in 1994, there were a lot of old sea dogs on board. We worked extremely hard, but the older guys treated us younger guys well and always footed the bill in port because we didn't earn much," he recalls nostalgically. "With reefer vessels, we brought back bananas from Ecuador, Colombia and the Caribbean as well as pineapples from South Africa and kiwis from New Zealand and Australia. It was fantastic! And everywhere we went, we were given huge palettes of fruit as gifts."

______ Less paperwork, more Christmas with "Home Alone"

One unforgettable memory involves Carnival and the 2014 FIFA World Cup games in Rio. "The laytimes were long, so we

verändert, sei schwer zu beurteilen, so der Kapitän: „Vielleicht wird es mit dem Papierkram doch mal wieder einfacher und bestimmt überlegen sich einige Firmen, ob sich nicht doch mehr Business online erledigen lässt – wer weiß?" Viel wichtiger ist für den Mann, der mitten in der Pandemie befördert wurde, dass er Weihnachten zu Hause ist. Und rückblickend auf Weihnachten letztes Jahr sagt er: „Es war wie immer sehr feierlich – ein Weihnachtsfest mit allem Drum und Dran. Und wie jedes Jahr haben wir am späten Abend „Kevin – Allein zu Haus", geschaut, das hat in ganz Polen Tradition!"

Hapag-Lloyd pflegt eine No-Blame-Kultur, das schätze ich sehr

could really join in the celebrations. You disembarked without any big controls and simply came back at some point." It was during this time that he got to experience what he had admired and envied as a boy about his brother, who is 10 years older than him. "We lived in Poland behind the Iron Curtain, but he was allowed to get out and he brought back stories and gifts from around the world."

When asked what the future holds and how the pandemic will change shipping, the captain says it's hard to say. "Maybe paperwork will become easier again, and I'm sure some companies are thinking about whether more business can be done online. Who knows?" Much more important for this man who was promoted in the midst of the pandemic is being home for the Christmas holidays. And looking back on last Christmas, he says: "Like always, it was very festive – a Christmas with all the frills. And, like every year, we watched 'Home Alone' in the late evening, which is a tradition in all of Poland!"

Was macht Sylwester Mackiewicz heute? Nach der Werftzeit mit der „Al Bahia" in Bremerhaven fuhr Sylwester Mackiewicz Einsätze auf der „Al Safat" (7.000 TEU), der „Umm Salal" (13.000 TEU) und ein weiteres Mal auf der „Al Safat" im SEC-Dienst (USA–Südamerika). Im September 2022 stieg er nach viereinhalb Monaten Fahrt in New York ins Flugzeug – und genießt jetzt die freie Zeit mit seiner Familie.

What's Sylwester Mackiewicz doing today? After being with the "Al Bahia" in Bremerhaven for a dry dock overhaul, Machiewicz sailed on the "Al Safat" (7,000 TEU), the "Umm Salal" (13,000 TEU) and again on the "Al Safat" on the SEC service (USA–South America). In September 2022, he boarded a plane in New York after a four-and-a-half-month voyage – and is now enjoying some time off with his family.

CONTAINER TERMINAL ALTENWERDER
CONTAINER TERMI
Hapag-Lloyd
BULK HAUL
BULK HAUL
g-Lloyd
g-Lloyd
seaco
eco container
ZPMC
KYOTO EXPRESS
Hapag-Lloyd
Hapag-Lloyd
Hapag-Lloyd

CONTAINER TERMINAL AL
TENWERDER
HHLA
Hapag-Lloyd
UASC
ZPMC
CTA
MILAN EXPRESS
HAMILTON

Impressum

Ein Gesamtverzeichnis der lieferbaren Titel
schicken wir Ihnen gerne zu.
Bitte senden Sie eine E-Mail mit Ihrer Adresse
an: vertrieb@koehler-books.de

Sie finden uns auch im Internet unter:
www.koehler-books.de

Bibliografische Information der Deutschen
Nationalbibliothek
Die Deutsche Nationalbibliothek verzeichnet
diese Publikation in der Deutschen
Nationalbibliografie;
detaillierte bibliografische Daten sind im
Internet über https://portal.dnb.de abrufbar.

ISBN 978-3-7822-1509-1

Texte:
Ulrike Fischer, Hamburg

Fotos:
Axel Martens, Hamburg
Uwe Fiedler, Hamburg (Seiten 124–131)

Lektorat:
Anke Taubitz, Hamburg

Übersetzung:
Josh Ward, Berlin

Gestaltung:
Jan Haux, Berlin

Druck & Bindung:
Plump Druck & Medien GmbH
Rolandsecker Weg 33
53619 Rheinbreitbach
www.mhp-print.de